Battle for the Falklands (2)

Naval Forces

Adrian English & Anthony Watts

Series editor Martin Windrow

Osprey Publishing, Elms Court, Chapel Way, Botley, Oxford
OX2 9LP, United Kingdom.
Email: info@ospreypublishing.com

Battle for the Falklands.—(Men-at-Arms series; 134)
   2: Naval forces
   1. Falkland Island War, 1982
   I. English, Adrian   II. Watts, Tony   III. Series
   997.11   F3031
ISBN 0-85045-492-1

Filmset in England by
Tameside Filmsetting Limited
Ashton-under-Lyne, Lancashire

Printed in China through World Print Ltd.

FOR A CATALOGUE OF ALL BOOKS PUBLISHED BY
OSPREY MILITARY AND AVIATION PLEASE CONTACT:

The Marketing Manager, Osprey Direct UK,
PO Box 140, Wellingborough, Northants,
NN8 4ZA, United Kingdom.
Email: info@ospreydirect.co.uk

The Marketing Manager, Osprey Direct USA,
c/o Motorbooks International, PO Box 1, Osceola,
WI 54020-0001, USA.
Email: info@ospreydirectusa.com

www.ospreypublishing.com

Editor's note:
Osprey Publishing Ltd wish to express their gratitude
to Geoff Cornish, Alexis Dunstan, Paul Haley, Lt. Cdr.
Ian Inskip, and John Moore for their assistance in the
preparation of this book. They also feel that it may be
desirable, under the circumstances, to note that a
donation has been made to the South Atlantic Fund.

Introduction

The 1,813 inhabitants of the Falkland Islands, who had gone to bed on the night of 1 April 1982—the Feast of All Fools—happy in the knowledge that they remained among the last and most remote bastions of the British Empire, awoke on 2 April to find that they had become unwilling citizens of Argentina. In the early hours of the chilly late-autumn morning substantial forces of Argentine Marines, with heavy naval and air support, had invaded the islands, quickly and almost bloodlessly overwhelming a token garrison of Royal Marines temporarily swollen to 67 by the early arrival of its relief detachment. The humour of Argentina's April Fool joke went largely unappreciated.

The following day Argentine forces also invaded the Falklands dependency of South Georgia, forcing the garrison of just 22 Royal Marines to surrender—though not before they had inflicted disproportionately heavy losses on their attackers.

When the Argentine military Junta led by Gen. Leopoldo Galtieri embarked upon the invasion as a solution to its multiple domestic political and economic problems, the auspices for its success

HMS *Endurance*—**her withdrawal to save £2m., announced in March 1982, probably had a direct effect on the Argentine decision to invade. With her bright red hull and almost non-existent on-board armament, she was forced to play cat and mouse around the islands until the arrival of the Task Force. Her MARISAT satellite communications system provided a valuable link with the UK during the campaign; and one of her Wasp helicopters saw action at South Georgia. (MoD)**

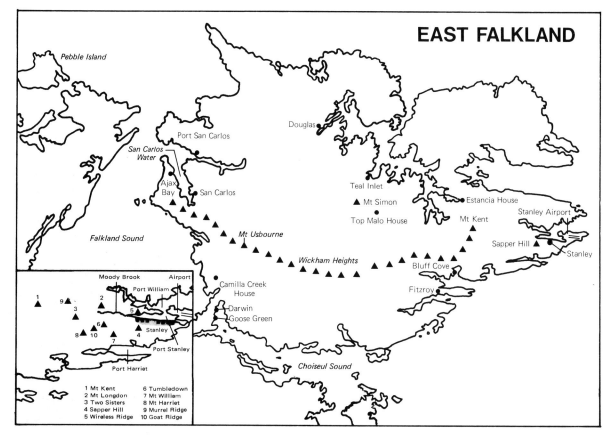

EAST FALKLAND

1 Mt Kent   6 Tumbledown
2 Mt Longdon   7 Mt William
3 Two Sisters   8 Mt Harriet
4 Sapper Hill   9 Murrel Ridge
5 Wireless Ridge   10 Goat Ridge

appeared to be singularly promising. Following 37 years of progressive disentanglement from its colonial past, Britain had reduced its overseas possessions to a handful of obscure islands and continental enclaves, most of them retained only in response to the wishes of a majority, at least, of their inhabitants to remain under British rule in preference to that of their immediate neighbours. Many of these survivals of Empire had become a nagging economic, if not a political embarassment to the British Foreign and Commonwealth Office.

The Falklands fulfilled these conditions to an extreme degree. For almost 20 years successive British governments had sought a formula which would permit the transfer of these barren and windswept rocks and peat bogs to the Argentines, while safeguarding the rights of the islanders. The Falklanders, although increasingly dependent on Argentina for materials, communications, and the practical needs of life, continued to display an understandable reluctance to exchange the sovereignty of a remote and rather uninterested democracy for the embrace of a neighbour where the military coup d'etat was a more usual

instrument of political change than the ballot box, and where political opponents of the current regime tended to disappear without trace.

While the stubborn desire of the islanders to remain British continued to pose a major obstacle to the long-drawn diplomatic discussions over sovereignty of the Falklands, and while practical links with Britain continued to erode, the British military presence in the South Atlantic was confined to a single platoon of some 40 Royal Marines at Stanley, the Falklands' tiny capital, and the 3,600-ton Antarctic patrol vessel HMS *Endurance*. Defence cuts announced in June 1981 by British Defence Secretary John Nott included the withdrawal of *Endurance* from service without replacement, and thus the end of any permanent British naval presence in the area. The path to military annexation of the islands without the risk of a significant British response seemed clear; and on his assumption of office in December 1981 Gen. Galtieri had announced that the Argentine flag would fly over the 'Islas Malvinas' before the 150th anniversary of their annexation by Britain came round in 1983.

4

The Invasion

Although the Argentine invasion of 2-3 April took the British government and apparently most of the rest of the world by surprise, it should not have done so. While Galtieri's remarks might have been dismissed as Latin bombast, warning signals of impending military action had been perceptible since February. In March a C-130 transport of the Argentine Air Force made an 'emergency' landing at Stanley, but took off again after proving that the runway of the only airport on the islands could handle heavy transport machines.

Early in March permission had been given to an Argentine scrap dealer, one Constantine Sergio Davidoff, to dismantle the derelict whaling station at Leith on South Georgia. On 18 March the Argentine Navy transport *Bahia Buen Suceso* landed a party of 42 'civilians', including some Marines, at Leith. They did not comply with the simple but legalistically important immigration formalities, and ran up the Argentine flag. Thirty of them later sailed away on the transport, but the flag continued to fly. HMS *Endurance* landed 22 Royal Marines at Leith with a 'watching brief'; and the Argentine polar transport *Bahia Paraiso* later landed additional supplies for their party before anchoring nearby.

At this delicate stage of what Britain and the world saw as a faintly comic dispute, on 28 March, an Argentine naval task force left the principal base at Puerto Belgrano, allegedly to take part in exercises with the Uruguayan Navy. It comprised the aircraft carrier *Veinticinco de Mayo*, the Type 42 destroyer *Hercules*, two old ex-US Navy destroyers *Segui* and *Comodoro Py*, the landing ship *Cabo San Antonio*, and three transports. Simultaneously, two French-built missile corvettes, *Drummond* and *Granville*, also sailed for South Georgia to support the *Bahia Paraiso*. Instead of heading north for Uruguay the main task force sailed south-east for the Falklands. On the night of 1 April it arrived in Falklands waters.

The initial Argentine landing was from rubber assault boats, by Commando frogmen who secured the lighthouse at Cape Pembroke, some seven miles from Stanley and marking the entrance to the harbour. They were followed by some 300 Marines

Some of the considerable modifications made to the cruiser *General Belgrano* **can be seen here: note two quadruple Sea Cat SAM launchers on bridge wings, Dutch LW08 surveillance radar forard and DA radar aft. The Sea Cat launchers were controlled by two Italian RTN10 FC systems. When HMS** *Conqueror's* **two World War II-vintage Mk 8 torpedos hit her on the port side, one amidships and one near the bows, the bow collapsed and folded down almost to the 6in. gun turret; the second torpedo appeared to have broken her back. (Dr. R. Scheina via MARS)**

in landing craft from the *Cabo San Antonio* who landed at Cape Pembroke and fanned out to take the airport, the runways of which had been blocked with vehicles. Elements of this force then deployed to link up with amphibious forces coming ashore from landing craft in Stanley harbour. Meanwhile the spearhead of the attack had landed from eight Sea King helicopters from the carrier, at Mullet Creek—150 Marine Commandos, who were soon followed by another 70 near the Royal Marine barracks at Moody Brook. A further 200 men came ashore, without significant resistance, in 16 LVTP-7 amphibious APCs, soon reinforced by landing craft.

After a three-hour resistance during which they disabled an LVTP, killed at least three of the enemy and wounded several times that number, the little garrison bowed to the inevitable and obeyed orders from the governor to surrender; the Argentines now had over 1,000 men ashore, with additional reinforcements arriving by the minute. Within 24 hours over 4,000 Argentines had landed.

The following day the 22 British defenders of

Veinticinco de Mayo **has been extensively modified over the years. She is currently fitted with the Ferranti CAAIS action information system modified for aircraft control functions, and giving computer–computer radio data links with the ANA's two new Type 42 destroyers. A recent refit gave her a catapult capable of launching the Super Etendard, and deck park space for three extra aircraft. Recently she has been operating up to 12 Skyhawks, five Trackers and four Sea Kings. After an inconclusive foray early in May, she is consistently reported to have been confined to base, ostensibly with engine trouble. (Dr. R. Scheina via MARS)**

The ANA submarine *Santiago del Estero,* **sister-ship to the ill-fated** *Santa Fé.* **Argentine submarine operations during the war are shrouded in secrecy; one claim has it that in all seven torpedos were fired, but that which missed the already-burning HMS** *Sheffield* **is the only one confirmed in available reports. In any event, no British ship was successfully attacked. (Dr. R. Scheina via MARS)**

South Georgia were overwhelmed. Before Lt. Keith Mills surrendered, his men had shot down at Alouette III and a Puma helicopter, killed between ten and 15 of the enemy, and inflicted serious damage on the *Granville* with anti-tank rockets. Meanwhile the *Endurance*, armed only with two 20mm cannon and two Wasp helicopters, waited

out at sea, and for a while she continued to shadow the *Bahia Paraiso*.

In response to one of the greatest national humiliations of recent times, Britain immediately severed diplomatic relations with Argentina and froze Argentine assets in the British financial world. A vigorous complaint at the breach of international law was lodged with the United Nations Security Council, which the following day passed by ten votes to one Resolution 502, condemning the Argentine aggression, calling for the immediate withdrawal of the invaders, and enjoining Britain and Argentina to seek a diplomatic solution to their differences. A week later the EEC voted unanimously to impose economic sanctions on Argentina, and to ban the delivery of military equipment to the Junta.

In their obvious expectation that Britain's response would be confined to diplomatic and economic measures, the Argentine Junta was gravely mistaken. (One is tempted to add that it was a mistake which could have been avoided by the most superficial study of the political career of Prime Minister Mrs. Margaret Thatcher.) An extraordinary session of the British Parliament on 3 April gave the government a predictably hard time; but all parties agreed that such a breach of international law could not go unavenged, and expressed almost unanimous support for the despatch of a naval task force, reservations being expressed only by the extreme and traditionally pacifist Left of the Labour Party. Two days later the concensus view that the disaster had been the responsibility of the Foreign and Commonwealth Office was marked by Mrs. Thatcher's acceptance of the resignation of the Foreign Secretary, Lord Carrington, and two of his subordinate ministers.

The Opposing Forces

While it was easy for politicians to make war-like noises, it was not so readily apparent how such noises could be translated into military credibility. The Falklands, only 400 miles from Argentina, were 8,000 miles from Britain, and 6,000 from Gibraltar, Britain's nearest base. The Royal Navy, continuously run down since 1945, was but a shadow of its former glory, when it had equalled the combat fleets of the rest of the world combined. It had suffered particularly severely from the 1981 defence cuts, which were designed to reduce it to an

The *Hercules* (D28) is of the British Type 42 destroyer class, but differs in mounting two MM.38 Exocet launchers atop the hangar aft since a 1980 refit, and has different EW equipment. (Vickers SB Ltd via MARS)

anti-submarine force scarcely adequate to defend the eastern half of the North Atlantic sea-route, the life-line of NATO in the event of an East–West confrontation. Fortunately, the projected cuts had not yet been implemented, and a fairly impressive fleet remained.

There were two anti-submarine aircraft carriers, 16 destroyers, 44 frigates and 31 submarines, of which about a dozen frigates and a similar number of submarines were either undergoing extensive refits or were 'moth-balled' in reserve, requiring several months work for re-activation. The amphibious assault force consisted of two assault ships and six logistic landing ships, plus about 60 minor non-ocean-going landing craft which were irrelevant in the prevailing situation. The 1981 cuts called for the reduction of the total number of destroyers and frigates to 50, and the disposal of the two amphibious assault ships (although both were subsequently reprieved). The run-down of the Royal Navy is best emphasised by pointing out that even during the Suez crisis of 1956 it had at its disposal no less than 14 carriers, 20 cruisers, 68 destroyers, 186 frigates, 54 submarines, 30 landing ships and 36 major landing craft.

The Argentine Navy, which had been the premier navy in Latin America since it had won a naval arms race with Chile at the turn of the century, had been nudged into second place by Brazil during the late 1960s. It remained relatively formidable in local terms, however, and had actually narrowed the gap between itself and the Royal Navy due to the latter's decline. In April 1982 it included one carrier, one cruiser, eight destroyers, five frigates and four submarines, with a

further four destroyers, six frigates and six submarines under construction. Rather ironically, its major amphibious warfare unit, the LSD *Candido de Lasala*, had been disposed of six months before the Falklands adventure; but demonstrably adequate sea-lift and amphibious assault capacity remained in the shape of two landing ships and six transports under naval command.

The Royal Navy

The major units of the Royal Navy were the carriers *Hermes* and *Invincible*. The 24,000-ton *Hermes* had been laid down as a light fleet carrier in 1944, but had suffered a delay in completion until 1959 while many design changes had been carried out. She was converted to a Commando carrier in 1971/73, and to a hybrid Commando/ASW carrier in 1976/77. A further refit in 1980 equipped her to carry Harrier 'jump-jets', the usual complement being five of these and nine Sea King ASW helicopters. She was scheduled for scrapping in 1984, although the Chilean Navy had evinced an interest in her. The 16,000-ton *Invincible*, the first of a class of three ASW carriers of a new type (originally designated 'through-deck cruisers' to hoodwink a pacifist-inclined Labour Party into voting funds for their construction) normally carried a similar complement of aircraft. Their initial air groups for the Falklands campaign were five Sea Harriers of No.801 Naval Air Squadron and five of No.899

The Rothesay class ASW frigate HMS *Plymouth* played a major part in the campaign, being involved in the capture of South Georgia and suffering major bomb damage at San Carlos, which put her out of action for four days. This photo was taken some time before the campaign, in the Far East. (MoD)

NAS on *Invincible*, and six each from Nos.800 and 899 NAS on *Hermes*. Although the only new carrier to join the fleet for years, *Invincible* was then destined for sale to Australia once her two sister-ships *Illustrious* and *Ark Royal* were completed.

Of the 16 destroyers, six were equipped with surface-to-surface and surface-to-air missiles, the remaining ten having only SAMs in addition to their guns and ASW armament. Of these the three Type 22s—*Broadsword*, *Battleaxe* and *Brilliant*, completed in 1979/81—displaced 3,500 tons and each mounted four Exocet SSMs, two six-barrelled Sea Wolf SAM launchers, and two Bofors 40mm/L60 AA guns. In addition, *Brilliant* had two triple Mk 32 anti-submarine torpedo tubes; and each carried either one or two Lynx helicopters—potent weapons in their own right, capable of carrying either ASMs or ASW torpedos.

The three surviving members of the 'County' Class—*Antrim*, *Glamorgan* and *Fife*, since *London* had been sold to Pakistan and *Norfolk* to Chile—had been completed in 1966/70 and displaced 5,400 tons. They carried four Exocet SSMs, a twin Sea Slug and two quadruple Sea Cat SAMs, a twin 4.5in. gun, two 20mm Oerlikons, and a Wessex ASW helicopter which could double as a 'battle taxi' for a squad of 16 Royal Marines.

Of the other destroyers, the 6,100-ton *Bristol*, completed in 1973, mounted a twin Sea Dart SAM launcher, an Ikara anti-submarine launcher, a single 4.5in. and two 20mm guns, and had a landing platform for a Wasp helicopter, although one was not normally carried. The nine 3,500-ton Type 42s—*Sheffield*, *Birmingham*, *Newcastle*, *Glasgow*,

General pre-war views of two Amazon class frigates, HMS
Ambuscade (**F172**) and *Alacrity* (**F174**), both of which served with the
Task Force. Following losses in the Falklands this class has
been severely criticised for the extensive use of aluminium in
the superstructure. Heavily armed for their size, they had
recourse to this light alloy construction to counter a possible
loss of stability due to this extra top-weight. Despite their
losses, these frigates performed valuable service under very
arduous conditions. Although their Exocet missiles were not
used, their guns, Sea Cat SAMs aft, and Lynx helicopters were
in constant use. (MoD)

Exeter, Southampton, Liverpool, Cardiff and *Coventry*, all
completed in 1975/82—each mounted a twin Sea
Dart, a single 4.5in. and two 20mm guns, and two
triple ASW torpedo tubes, and carried a Lynx
helicopter. The future of six more Type 42s at
various stages of construction hung in the balance,
although three additional Type 22s were to be
completed and a seventh ordered. The surviving
'County' Class ships were to be disposed of within
the next three years.

The British frigate force included the eight 2,750-
ton Type 21s, completed in 1974/78; *Amazon,
Antelope, Active, Ambuscade, Arrow, Alacrity, Ardent* and
Avenger each mounted four Exocets, a quadruple
Sea Cat, one 4.5in. and two 20mm guns, and two
triple ASW torpedo tubes, and carried a Lynx or
Wasp helicopter. The 26 'Leander' Class ships fell
into three distinct categories: Group I, ASW vessels
armed with Ikara forward; Group II, armed with

Exocet and Sea Cat forward; and Group III,
mounting either twin 4.5in. guns forward and
Limbo ASW launchers aft, or four Exocets and Sea
Wolf forward. For individual details of these ships,
displacing 2,450 tons and completed in 1974/81, see
the table at the back of this book. The ten
'Rothesay' Class frigates, from which the former
type were developed, displaced 2,380 tons and were
completed in 1960/61. They mounted a quadruple
Sea Cat, a twin 4.5in., and a triple Limbo ASW
mortar, and carried a Lynx or Wasp. The
'Leanders' and 'Rothesays' were to be phased out of
service by the mid-1980s, although the construction
of an as-yet undesigned Type 23 class was
envisaged.

The real sting of the slimmed-down Royal Navy
lay in its submarines, of which the four 7,500-ton
nuclear powered 'Resolutions', completed in
1967/69, carried 16 Polaris nuclear missiles apiece
in addition to six torpedo tubes. There were 11
other nuclear powered attack submarines: the six
'Swiftsures', built in 1978/81; the two 'Valiants',
built in 1966/67; and the three 'Churchills',
completed in 1970/71. All of these vessels were in the
4,200–4,400 ton surface displacement range, and
mounted five or six torpedo tubes. In addition there
were 13 diesel/electric 'Oberons' and three
'Porpoises', all completed between 1958 and 1967,

all displacing 2,000 tons surfaced, and all mounting eight torpedo tubes. Submarines were the only growth area in the Nott plans, the nuclear powered attack force being scheduled to rise to 17; and there was provision for a new class of conventionally powered hunter-killers to supplement and eventually supercede the 'Oberons' and 'Porpoises'.

The two assault ships *Intrepid* and *Fearless*, completed in 1965/67 to a design based on the American LSD, displaced 11,000 tons and carried eight smaller landing craft, with facilities for up to five Wessex helicopters, to disembark a maximum of 700 troops with their equipment. They carried a defensive armament of a quadruple Sea Cat launcher and two 40mm guns. The six logistic landing craft were not true assault vessels, being designed for the support of an already secured beachhead; completed in 1966/67 and displacing 3,300 tons, they could carry 500 troops and their equipment and up to 20 helicopters each. They were named *Sir Bedivere*, *Sir Lancelot*, *Sir Galahad*, *Sir Geraint*, *Sir Percival* and *Sir Tristram*.

Among the minor vessels of the Royal Navy were three new 600-ton minehunters with six similar ships under construction; plus 33 smaller and older minesweepers and hunters dating back to the early 1950s, and 20 assorted patrol craft. More importantly, there was a comprehensive fleet train of six large fleet tankers and four fleet replenishment ships, plus two stores support ships and a multiplicity of smaller tankers, water carriers, stores ships and tugs, permitting the fleet to operate far

HMS *Invincible*, **whose air cover and ASW capability was of central importance to the Task Force. Her normal complement (five Sea Harriers of No. 801 NAS and nine Sea Kings of No. 820) was increased during the campaign by three Sea Harriers of No. 899 NAS and two of No. 809, and at least one extra Sea King was carried. The Sea Harriers in the stern view carry both the all-over dark sea grey scheme of the original complement, and in two cases the lighter grey scheme used by No. 809. The self-defence capability of** *Invincible* **was woefully inadequate; the forard Sea Dart virtually duplicates the role of the aircraft, and close-in systems such as Sea Wolf have been totally lacking. (MoD)**

from its bases for extended periods.

This fleet was manned by a total of 74,000 all ranks, men and women, including just under 8,000 Royal Marines whose major units comprised three battalion-sized Commandos, a Special Boat Squadron and two Raiding Squadrons. Naval personnel were scheduled for cuts of 10,000 by the mid-1980s.

Despite the abandonment of the conventional fleet aircraft carrier the Fleet Air Arm retained a fairly impressive inventory of about 500 principally rotary-winged aircraft. There were scheduled to be 34 Sea Harrier V/STOL jet fighter-bombers in five squadrons, of which one was a training unit; 94 Sea King ASW and assault helicopters in six operational and one training squadrons; 150 Wessex, in three training, one assault and one general purpose squadrons plus two ASW flights; 88 Lynx, in one training squadron and 23 ASW flights; 80 Wasps, in one training squadron and 22 ASW flights; plus small numbers of other fixed and rotary-winged communications and training types.

Argentina's Naval Forces

The principle surface unit of the Argentine Navy was the 16,000-ton, thrice-modernised light fleet

Units of the Task Force head south towards Ascension Island: from nearest, they are HMS Glamorgan, Broadsword, Alacrity *and* Yarmouth. *(MoD)*

The troopship SS *Canberra* refuels from the RFA *Tidespring* using the abeam transfer method. During a short refit before sailing the liner was fitted with two helicopter landing stations, which can be seen over the forard swimming pool and aft of the bridge, as well as replenishment equipment. (MoD)

Seen from HMS *Antrim*, HMS *Plymouth* opens fire on enemy positions at Grytviken in South Georgia on 25 April during the action to recapture the dependency. (MoD)

carrier ARA *Veinticinco de Mayo*, completed as HMS *Venerable* in 1945 and originally a 'half-sister' to HMS *Hermes*. Sold to the Netherlands in 1948 as HrMS *Karel Doorman*, she was sold third-hand to Argentina in 1968 to replace an earlier and similar carrier, ARA *Independencia*. Normally carrying 12 Douglas A-4Q Skyhawks, six Grumman Tracker ASW aircraft and four Sea Kings, *Veinticinco de Mayo* took part in the Falklands invasion with a temporarily doubled complement of helicopters. She had a defensive armament of ten 40mm guns, and extensive modern electronic equipment of Dutch origin.

Second largest ship in the Argentine fleet, but of greatly diminished military importance, was the cruiser ARA *General Belgrano*. Completed in 1939 and the last survivor of the Japanese attack on Pearl Harbor, the 11,000-ton *General Belgrano* had been acquired in 1951, together with a sister-ship, *Nueve de Julio*, scrapped in 1979. With an armour belt varying from 1.5 to 4 inches and deck armour varying from 2 to 3 inches, the 43 year-old *Belgrano* was one of very few armoured ships still afloat. Her main armament consisted of 15×6in. guns in five triple turrets, eight single 5in. and two twin 40mm guns, plus two quadruple Sea Cat SAM launchers. The old ship also carried two helicopters.

The most modern major surface vessels of the fleet were the destroyers *Hércules* and *Santísima Trinidad*, ironically enough British Type 42 vessels,

the former built in Britain and the latter in Argentina. The *Hércules* had in fact been built in the neighbouring construction bay to HMS *Sheffield*, with which she helpfully exchanged engines when those of the latter were damaged by fire. As recently as the beginning of March 1982 *Santísima Trinidad* had been carrying out missile firing trials at the Ministry of Defence range at Aberporth in Wales.

Argentina also had six old ex-US Navy destroyers. These included the 2,400-ton *Comodoro Py* of the 'Gearing' Class, completed in 1945 and transferred in 1973; modified to FRAM II standards, the *Py* carried four single Exocet launchers in addition to her two twin 5in. guns, two triple ASW torpedo tubes, and two Hedgehog anti-submarine weapons, and was equipped to handle a small helicopter. Slightly smaller were the three 2,200-ton 'Allen M. Sumner' Class destroyers *Seguí*, *Hipólito Bouchard* and *Piedrabuena*, the latter two also modified to FRAM II standards before transfer in 1972. All completed in 1944, these ships each mounted four Exocets and three twin 5in. guns, two triple ASW torpedo tubes and two Hedgehogs, and the latter two could handle a helicopter. *Seguí*, acquired in 1974, had no helicopter facility, but carried two twin 3in. AA guns. Finally, there were the 39 year-old 'Fletcher' Class *Rosales* and *Almirante Storni*, transferred in 1971 and each mounting four single 5in. guns, three twin 3in. AA guns, two triple ASW torpedo tubes and two Hedgehogs. Four

An Amazon class frigate in the South Atlantic. Sea conditions were reasonable for much of the campaign, although cold and windy; wind rarely exceeded Force 8 (34/40kts). Occasional winds of Force 9 to 10 (55 + kts) created a swell up to 33ft., however, which combined with 20-ft. waves to produce swells up to 50ft. The worst problem was the length and depth of the swell, and at some moments even *Invincible* was heaving and falling 30ft. every ten seconds. With temperatures of −3°C and 55kt winds conditions in the open could be lethal, as windchill factor effectively cut the temperature to −15°C. This photo shows clearly the 4.5in. Mk 8 fully automatic gun which saw a great deal of use in the Falklands; at least one frigate wore out its tube giving naval gunfire support. (Tom Smith, Daily Express)

3,600-ton Meko Type 360 destroyers were under construction in Germany, the first three being actually in the water, and the first being scheduled for commission in July 1982.

The escort force was completed by the French-built Type A69 light frigates *Drummond*, *Guerrico* and *Granville*, and the locally-built *Murature* and *King*, both used for training. The first two Type A69s had been ordered for South Africa but purchased by Argentina when delivery was halted by the UN arms embargo. Completed in 1978, these were followed by the third vessel in 1981. Of just under 1,000 tons displacement, the A69s each mounted four single Exocets; a 3.9in., a twin 40mm and two 20mm guns, and two triple ASW torpedo tubes. The other ships were enlarged versions of a class of minesweepers built in Argentina in the late 1930s, themselves based on a German First World War design. Completed in 1945 and 1946, these 1,000-ton vessels mounted three single 4.1in. and four single 40mm guns; and were of minimal value in the conditions of modern naval warfare. Six Meko Type 140 1,700-ton light frigates were also building, in local yards, with German assistance.

The submarine force consisted of the 1,200-ton surface displacement *Salta* and *San Luis*, of the German Type 209 class, both completed in 1974 and mounting eight torpedo tubes; and the 37 year-old ex-US 'Guppy' Class *Santa Fé* and *Santiago del Estero*, both of 1,900 tons and mounting ten torpedo tubes, acquired in 1971. Two 1,700-ton and two 2,100-ton submarines were to be built in Argentina for completion in 1983/84, with an additional two of the larger type under construction in Germany.

The main amphibious assault strength of the Argentine Navy consisted of the 4,300-ton landing ship *Cabo San Antonio*, completed in Argentina in 1978; designed to carry two smaller landing craft and a helicopter, she had three quadruple 40mm AA guns. Further sea-lift capacity was provided by the three 4,600-ton transports *Canal Beagle*, *Bahia San Blas* and *Cabo de Hornos*, all completed in Argentina in 1978/79; the 32-year-old Canadian-built *Bahia Aguirre* and *Bahia Buen Suceso* of 3,100 tons; and the 37-year-old, 2,400-ton ex-US LST *Cabo San Pio*. There were also about three dozen small landing craft of little relevance to the Falklands campaign. The 9,000-ton polar transport *Bahia Paraiso* and the 12,000-ton icebreaker *Almirante Irizar* were also available for logistic support, the former taking part in the invasion of South Georgia, and both subsequently serving as hospital ships.

The Argentine Navy also possessed two German-built 200-ton fast attack craft and four Israeli-built 'Dabur' Class coastal patrol craft, all of which were stationed in southern waters, where they appear to have remained—although propaganda film purporting to show them operating off the Falklands was widely shown. There were also five armed tugs used as patrol vessels. Six British-built 'Ton' Class minesweeper/hunters provided the nucleus of a mine warfare force. Finally, there was a modest but useful fleet train, of which the most significant unit was the 14,400-ton replenishment tanker *Punta Medanos*, completed in Britain in 1950.

This fleet was manned by a total of 36,000 all ranks, including a naval air arm of 3,000 and a Marine Corps of 10,000. (Details of the air and land forces of the Navy will be found where relevant in the accompanying titles, MAA 133: 'Land Forces' and MAA 135: 'Air Forces'.) Also coming under naval command was a coastguard force, the 9,000-man Prefectura Naval, with ten large patrol vessels of over 100 tons, about 30 smaller craft, and an air wing of five Skyvan light transports and three Puma and six Hughes 500 helicopters. Elements of this organisation were deployed to the Falklands.

* * *

While the balance of forces appeared to give an overwhelming superiority to the Royal Navy, the Argentine Junta obviously calculated that in the context of its NATO commitment only a relatively small proportion of available forces could be detached to the South Atlantic, where its true function would be to strengthen Britain's hand at the negotiating table. The idea that a country which had given away the greatest empire in history would actually fight for one of its few remaining colonial liabilities was not worthy of serious contemplation. In this assessment of the British national mood, and of the realities of British political life, the Junta were sorely mistaken.

The liner *QE2*, used to transport 5 Inf. Bde., was thought too valuable to be risked in 'Bomb Alley'; she transferred her troops at South Georgia, where she is shown here with the requisitioned trawler *Northella*, used as a minesweeper, alongside. (MoD)

The crippled *Santa Fé* lying in Grytviken harbour. Note the damage caused by AS.12 missiles as they ripped through the conning tower, taking strips of plating with them, and exploded on the starboard side. (MoD)

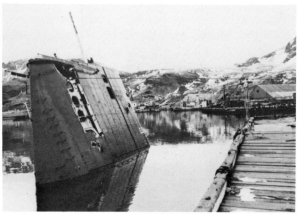

The Campaign

In the days following the invasion, Argentina mounted a massive air and sea-lift of personnel and material into the islands. About 40 per cent of the total Marine forces were already present. These were rapidly reinforced by naval, air, and surface elements. As early as 4 April a flight of four MB.339A light strike jets of the 1st Naval Attack Squadron, followed by T-34s of the 4th Naval Attack Squadron, were flown into Stanley airport, to be followed by additional elements of both units. While the major naval surface units which had

mounted the invasion returned to mainland bases within a matter of days, two armed tugs—*Alférez Sobral* and *Comodoro Somellera*—were deployed to the newly established Apostadero Naval Malvinas. Units of the Prefectura Naval, including at least four of the German-built 80-ton 'Z-28' Type patrol craft and a number of aircraft, were also posted to the islands. (Although details are sketchy at present, it is thought that at one time at least one Super Etendard was flown into Stanley.)

At first the islanders were treated with stiff correctness; but the hapless young conscripts, who found that the island paradise conjured up by propaganda was in fact a barren and windswept group of rocks, also found that any attempts at friendliness were rebuffed by islanders whom they had been led to believe would welcome them as saviours from colonial oppression. The Falklanders' worst fears of the consequences of Argentine occupation were soon confirmed. Only three days after the invasion the petty decrees imposing the Spanish language and metric measurements, and

HMS *Conqueror* **approaches her base at Faslane, Scotland on her return from the South Atlantic, and follows the old custom of flying a 'Jolly Roger' to mark a successful patrol against hostile forces. The centre motif is a skull on crossed torpedos; in the top fly corner is a white warship silhouette, marking the sinking of** *Belgrano*, **and in the top hoist corner is a white curved dagger shape, marking a successful clandestine mission—e.g. landing SBS men in enemy territory. The Leftist media made great play of the apparent 'bloodthirstiness' of the Jolly Roger, but the custom goes back more than 40 years and was adopted by all Allied submarines in World War II. (MoD via MARS)**

HMS *Sheffield* was the first major British warship lost as a direct result of enemy action since 1945. This was the first occasion that an airborne anti-ship missile had been used in action; the first use in action of Exocet; and the first operation in which a guided missile destroyer had been in action. The missile's entry hole can be seen at the base of the smoke-pall close to the waterline. Although it did not detonate, its passage through the ship fractured fuel lines, destroyed pumps controlling the water main, wrecked the control room, and ended in the damage control headquarters, where its fuel started raging fires which the crew were at first obliged to fight with water-buckets and hand-extinguishers for lack of anything better. Just visible on the bridge roof ahead of the radome is a large Union flag recognition sign, reminding us that Argentina also had Type 42 destroyers. (MoD)

driving on the right, were followed by altogether more sinister announcements. Martial law was declared, and heavy penalties were threatened for failure to show 'due respect' to the occupiers and their 'national symbols'. On 7 April Brig.Gen. Mario Benjamín Menéndez, an officer with a reputation for ruthless suppression of dissidents in north-west Argentina, was appointed military governor of the Malvinas Territory, as the Falklands were now officially termed in Argentina.

The Task Force Assembles

While the British government had largely misread the warning signals of impending invasion, a Royal Fleet Auxiliary tanker had been dispatched to the South Atlantic on 30 March, and plans for the assembly of a naval task force were already in hand when news of the invasion reached Britain three days later.

While the *Endurance* remained in the area, deliberately avoiding Argentine naval units for which her two puny 20mm guns would have been no match, the nearest British forces were a squadron

of 16 destroyers and frigates which had just completed a NATO exercise off Gibraltar. It was nevertheless announced that from 12 April Britain would enforce a Total Exclusion Zone within a 200-mile radius of the Falklands, and that any Argentine vessels found within that zone would be sunk. The instruments of this threat were rumoured to be two British nuclear attack submarines, *Superb* and *Spartan*, which were on station in the South Atlantic. This had the effect of persuading the major Argentine surface units to return to the mainland bases from which they seldom emerged thereafter; but it was pure bluff, since both submarines were at that time in the North Atlantic, and *Superb* was on her way home to her base at Faslane. (British submarine deployment is still subject to official secrecy, but it is believed that *Spartan* did later sail for the South Atlantic.)

The carriers *Hermes* and *Invincible*, together with the assault ship *Fearless*, were at Portsmouth—a dockyard scheduled to be downgraded under the Nott cuts—and were made ready for sea in the incredible space of three days. The task was done by dockyard personnel working round the clock, many of them with redundancy notices in their pockets. The logistic landing ship *Sir Geraint*, loaded with stores, had actually left Plymouth on the evening of 2 April, within hours of the news of the invasion. These ships were followed in quick succession by the fleet oilers *Tidespring*, *Olmeda*, *Appleleaf* and *Pearleaf* and the fleet replenishment ships *Fort Austin*, *Resource* and *Stromness*; the last-named, refitted as a troop transport in a matter of days, embarked part of 45 Cdo.RM. The Chilean Navy agreed to accept a delay in the delivery of the oiler *Tidepool*, sold to them two months earlier, and she once more hoisted her old flag to join the growing fleet. A former submariner, Rear Admiral John ('Sandy') Woodward, was rescued from a Whitehall desk to command the Task Force; by the time he joined his flagship *Hermes* at sea, by helicopter, the destroyers *Antrim*, *Glamorgan*, *Coventry*, *Glasgow*, *Sheffield*, *Battleaxe*, *Brilliant* and *Broadsword*, and the frigates *Ariadne*, *Plymouth* and *Yarmouth* had joined what one commentator was insensitive enough to describe as an 'armada'. This was already the largest fleet of British warships assembled since the Suez crisis of 1956. Ironically, many of the men who served in it had also been marked for redundancy in the near future.

The second assault ship, HMS *Intrepid*, already decommissioned and awaiting disposal, was rapidly brought back into service; together with the logistic landing ships *Sir Bedivere*, *Sir Galahad*, *Sir Lancelot*, *Sir Percival* and *Sir Tristram*.

As early as 4 April contingency plans were put in hand for the requisitioning of merchant ships to carry additional troops and equipment. The first to be taken over was the P & O cruise liner *Canberra*; her conversion into a troop ship began as soon as she docked at Southampton on 7 April, and as soon as was practicable she began embarking 40 and 42 Cdo.RM and 3rd Parachute Bn. She was followed by the container ship *Elk*, which loaded two Troops of the Blues and Royals (Royal Horse Guards) with their Scorpion and Scimitar tracked reconnaissance vehicles, and heavy bridging gear of the Royal Engineers. The *Europic* and *Norland* ferries embarked 2nd Parachute Bn.; and *Atlantic Conveyor* (a container ship converted into a make-shift aircraft carrier to transport 20 Harriers) was also pressed into service.

The liner *Uganda*, on an educational cruise in the Mediterranean, disembarked 1,000 school children at Gibraltar, where she was rapidly fitted out as a hospital ship. Also converted to serve as hospital ships were the naval surveying vessels *Hecla*, *Herald* and *Hydra*. The Royal Yacht *Britannia*, which has an alternative wartime role as a hospital ship, was not deployed to the South Atlantic, to the frustration of her crew. By mid-April a total of 31 merchant vessels—two passenger liners, three container ships, two other cargo vessels, 16 tankers, four large trawlers converted as minesweepers, an oil-rig tender for use as a repair ship, and three powerful tugs—had been pressed into naval service.

The War of Words

As the Task Force plodded southwards, its speed limited to that of its slowest elements, frantic diplomatic attempts to avoid armed conflict were in progress, chiefly under the auspices of the US government. The Anglo-Argentine confrontation placed the USA in an unenviable position, since it had treaty obligations to both parties, and common interests with both. While backing UN Resolution 502, the USA had stopped short of full economic sanctions or a total military embargo. The Soviet

This photo of the old target frigate *Undaunted*, after being struck forard by an Exocet fired on the range by HMS *Norfolk*, proves beyond question that the AM.39 which struck *Sheffield* on 4 May did not, in fact, explode. The damage done by a detonating Exocet warhead is shown here to be so gross that *Sheffield's* loss would have been much quicker, and her casualty list many times longer. (MoD via MARS)

Union and its Cuban satellite had given strong verbal support to Argentina, and the possibility of the affair escalating into a full-scale East-West confrontation could not be ruled out. In an effort to defuse a potentially explosive situation US Secretary of State Alexander Haig was despatched on an exhausting three-week shuttle mission between London and Buenos Aires, in an attempt to find some common ground for a settlement. While preserving a necessary semblance of neutrality, the US government nevertheless assisted Britain in a number of ways. The most useful and tangible form of support was the facility of the use of the US military air base at Ascension Island, a British possession approximately half way between Britain and the Falklands leased to the USA by the British government. Under existing arrangements the US also passed on intelligence information gained from spy satellites.

On 12 April, the day when the Total Exclusion Zone around the Falklands officially came into effect, the Task Force reached Ascension for much-needed replenishment. Twelve RAF Nimrod long-range maritime reconnaissance aircraft from Kinloss and St. Mawgan were sent to Ascension; and on 19 April it was announced that some of the

As *Sheffield* **burns, HMS** *Arrow* **lies close alongside pumping water in a vain attempt to contain her fires—which were so fierce that** *Arrow* **herself was in considerable danger. Capt. Salt decided to abandon ship after five hours of exhausting efforts to save her, when it became clear that the fire was out of control, and when it was known that enemy submarines were active—one torpedo had already been fired at** *Sheffield* **as she burned. Note broad black stripe painted from funnel to waterline on British Type 42s as a recognition measure. (MoD)**

RAF's Vulcan bombers, retired from service only weeks before, would be re-activated to carry out operations from Ascension. After four days at Ascension, spent refuelling, replenishing, embarking extra equipment flown out from Britain by RAF Hercules, and stretching the troops' legs, the Task Force resumed its voyage on 16 April.

Three days later the sighting of a submarine periscope caused the first alert, and the following day all ships of the Task Force went on to a war footing as they approached extreme flying range of Argentine land-based aircraft. Adm. Woodward had only 22 Sea Harriers at his disposal—12 crammed aboard *Hermes*, of which only eight could be operated simultaneously, and ten aboard *Invincible*, of which only five could operate at any one time. Lack of adequate air cover was to be the major preoccupation throughout the campaign; Argentina had a total of more than 130 modern fighters and fighter-bombers, as well as nine old Canberra bombers and over 100 light strike types.

Meanwhile, the Haig peace mission was foundering; on 23 April the new British Foreign Secretary, Francis Pym, flew to Washington to try to convince the US administration to come out unequivocally on Britain's side. On the same day Adm. Woodward announced the imposition of an air as well as a sea blockade throughout the TEZ, which the Task Force had now entered. On that same day the Task Force suffered its first casualty when a Sea King helicopter from *Hermes* ditched with the loss of one crewman.

Argentine aircraft, principally Boeing 707 transports, had been shadowing the Task Force since 20 April, as had the merchant ship *Rio de La Plata* until she was chased off by a frigate. These observers now noted that the Task Force had split into two elements, one of which headed southwards and the other east.

The Shooting War Begins
The smaller element, including the destroyer *Antrim*, the frigate *Plymouth* and the tanker *Tidespring* rendezvoused with the ice patrol ship *Endurance* off South Georgia on 22 April. (*Endurance* had remained in the vicinity of South Georgia since 3 April, maintaining a tenuous communications link with a party of British scientists on South Georgia, and with London via a satellite link.)

Although hard information is not available, it is believed that on the night of 20/21 April 12 men of the Royal Marines SBS were put ashore from the submarine *Onyx*. The manner of their arrival in the theatre of operations deserves comment; several days earlier they had parachuted into the icy sea from a Hercules transport, wearing scuba gear, to rendezvous with the submerged submarine and board her, while still submerged, by way of one of the escape hatches. The following day some 15 men of 22 SAS Regt. were also inserted, by Wessex helicopter, to reconnoitre. In blizzard conditions, with winds of 100mph, the helicopter crashed during an attempt to pick them up later the same day. A second Wessex, from *Tidespring*, also crashed. A third, from *Antrim*, finally succeeded in evacuating the SAS men, their weapons and equipment, and the stranded aircrew—an astonishing feat of airmanship, in appalling 'white-out' conditions, by Lt.Cdr. Ian Stanley, whose Wessex carried a gross overload of 17 men on the successful flight, his seventh mission in two days. Lt.Cdr. Stanley was awarded an immediate DSO.

On 24 April the SAS party again went ashore, this time from rubber boats, again without attracting the attention of the small garrison—a company of Argentine Marines.

The following morning the Wessex from *Antrim* and a Lynx from an 'Amazon' Class frigate, returning after a recce flight, spotted the Argentine submarine *Santa Fé* proceeding away from Grytviken harbour, where she had landed 40 Marine reinforcements. The Wessex closed, and dropped two depth charges close alongside, which did irreparable machinery damage although not actually holing the hull. This attack was followed up by another, by a Lynx from HMS *Brilliant*, after which the crippled submarine turned about and began limping back towards the island. At that point a Wasp from HMS *Endurance* attacked the *Santa Fé*, firing a number of AS.12 missiles; these passed through the thin plating of the conning tower and detonated on the other side, the plating having insufficient strength to detonate them on impact. Under these attacks, followed by machine gun runs, the crew eventually drove the submarine ashore and abandoned her.

Capitalising on the enemy's confusion, 120 men of 'M'Coy., 42 RM Cdo., supported by about 30 SAS troops, landed by helicopter under cover of bombardment by the 4.5in. guns of the naval vessels. After brief resistance the Argentine garrison surrendered, one being shot in error. In all 156 Argentine service personnel, including the crew of *Santa Fé* and its erstwhile passengers, plus 38 Argentine civilians, became prisoners. The surrender was formally signed aboard HMS *Plymouth* by Lt.Cdr. Alfredo Astiz, the garrison commander. A sinister figure, whose activities in the mid-1970s prompted the governments of both Sweden and France to request the opportunity to question him about the disappearance of their nationals—a 17-year-old girl and two elderly missionary nuns—allegedly at his hands, Astiz was not repatriated with the other prisoners. He was eventually flown to Britain, but a strict interpretation of the Geneva Convention unfortunately obliged Britain to release him. He reached Uruguay, but is reported to have disappeared there. The Argentine government displays no interest in this fact.

Filled with a justifiable pride at the satisfactory outcome of the first phase of the expulsion of the invaders, Adm. Woodward told a reporter with the Task Force: 'South Georgia was the appetiser. Now this is the heavy punch coming up behind. This is the run-up to the big match, which in my view should be a walk-over'. These ill-considered words from an officer unused to dealing with the Press—as are most Royal Navy, as opposed to British Army,

The burnt-out *Sheffield*, in which 20 men died, the youngest an 18-year-old cook. Taken in tow, she eventually went down on 10 May when the weather took a turn for the worse. (Martin Cleaver, Press Association)

Representative of the Royal Fleet Auxiliaries without which the campaign could not have been mounted, RFA *Stromness*; laid up at Portsmouth, she was refitted as a troopship in just three days, and took part of 45 Cdo.RM to the South Atlantic. (M G Photographic)

Sir Lancelot, one of the LSLs which proved so valuable; she ferried troops, and took part in the San Carlos landings. Heavily bombed on 24 May, and abandoned when an unexploded 1,000-pounder lodged deep in her hull, she was hit again on the 25th; she was reboarded when the bomb was made safe. The pale grey patch below the nearest lifeboat shows its entry hole. (Mike Lennon)

officers—were not well received in Westminster. Three days later Adm. Woodward modified his remarks, saying that there would be 'no simple, short, quick military solution' and that the campaign would probably be 'long and bloody'.

On 29 April Secretary Haig's final proposals to the Argentine Junta were rejected; and on the 30th the US government acknowledged the failure of diplomacy and announced its unequivocal support for Great Britain at any level short of participation by US personnel in military operations. Meanwhile, the Task Force continued to receive reinforcements. At least four submarines now patrolled the limits of the TEZ, and further ships continued to leave Britain for the South Atlantic, including the frigates *Active*, *Ardent* and *Avenger*, and two more Royal Fleet Auxiliaries.

Adm. Woodward's 'Big Match' was about to commence.

South Atlantic Conditions

This may be a logical point to digress briefly about the conditions faced by the ships, and the young men, of the Task Force.

When the Task Force set sail the South Atlantic was moving from autumn to winter—in the event, one of the mildest early winters on record for that area. Even so, conditions were still extremely dangerous, especially to those unused to operating in that part of the world. Although well accustomed by long training to operating in Arctic conditions, the Royal Navy and Royal Marines faced new hazards in the South Atlantic. There were gales reaching 100mph, whipping up waves of up to 50 feet, giving rise to some of the roughest waters in the world, with freezing spray which can coat everything it touches in ice—lethal to the unwary on board ship. Although this particular hazard was not so widespread as expected due to the mild winter, the water itself remained near freezing for much of the time; if a man fell in his chances of survival were slim unless he was picked up in minutes—assuming, of course, that he was wearing some kind of survival suit to start with. The coastal waters immediately around the Falklands are slightly warmer, giving a longer survival time. The islands produced a different hazard, however, and one not before experienced by British troops.

This was the combination of intense cold with fine, drenching rain, which could produce a chill factor of $-20°C$: far deadlier than the dry cold of the Arctic. Unless men are properly clothed, such a chill factor can very rapidly lead to severe hypothermia, and probably to death, among even the fittest troops. Apart from the cold and driving rain there were frequent snow storms, which gave rise to abominable conditions ashore.

The islands themselves resemble the Western Highlands of Scotland, although with lower hills. There are, however, quite a number of prominent

'Bomb Alley', 22 May: near-misses straddle ships of the landing force. Left to right: RFA *Olna*, ferry *Norland*, assault ship HMS *Intrepid*, RFA *Fort Austin*. (MoD)

features dotted about the terrain which played a prominent role in the ground fighting. They also provided excellent observation points from which the movement of shipping close inshore could be observed with ease—a factor of which the Task Force had to be keenly aware, especially during the early days of the campaign.

The Softening-Up Process

On the morning of 1 May (coincidentally, Adm. Woodward's 50th birthday) the airfield at Stanley was bombed, first before dawn by a single Vulcan, and later by Harriers from *Hermes* and *Invincible*. The grass air strip at Goose Green was also bombed, and a destroyer and two frigates commenced a bombardment of Argentine positions at Stanley, inflicting some casualties. A Sea King also strafed Argentine troops at Darwin, near the Goose Green air strip.

Argentine reaction was slow in coming and ill co-ordinated. Later that day six jets—Israeli-built Daggers and/or the very similar Mirage III—and several Canberra bombers attacked the Task Force, two fighters and one Canberra falling to the patrolling Sea Harriers and a third Mirage to the Argentines' own ground fire at Stanley. The frigate HMS *Arrow* suffered some damage from a bomb, one member of the crew receiving splinter wounds. The only other British casualty was a Sea Harrier which returned safely with a single hole through its fin.

The next day, 2 May, was a disastrous one for the Argentine Navy. The cruiser *General Belgrano*, escorted by the destroyers *Hipólito Bouchard* and *Piedrabuena*, was intercepted by the nuclear attack submarine *Conqueror* some 36 miles outside the TEZ. Acting on direct orders from London, *Conqueror* launched three torpedoes at the cruiser, one of which blew off her bows, another hitting her in the engine room.* She began to settle by the stern, sinking two hours later with the eventual loss of 321 of her crew of 1,042. Only in October did the government reveal that almost the whole enemy surface fleet was then at sea, approaching the TEZ; *Belgrano's* fate seems to have turned them round without any further encounters.

Whatever the military justification for sinking *Belgrano*, the failure to reveal the scope of the Argentine operation at the time was a political blunder of the greatest magnitude. Her sinking, in international waters, without a formal declaration of war and, as at first appeared, with the loss of nearly three times as many lives as was subsequently shown to be the case, caused a shudder of horror both in Britain and abroad. By this one stroke the British government had endangered its enormous moral advantage. To civilian observers overseas it seemed that the campaign to repossess the Falklands was being fought in an unreasonably bloodthirsty manner.

From the Argentine point of view, this deployment of an ancient ship, of very limited military potential in the conditions of modern

---

* Notwithstanding Press speculation about the capabilities of the Royal Navy's Tigerfish 21in. wire-guided electrically-propelled 3-D active/passive acoustic homing torpedo, with an estimated range of up to 32km, these were in fact Second World War vintage 21in. Mk 8 torpedos with magnetic pistol, compressed-air propulsion, and maximum range of 4,500m.

warfare, was a foretaste of the quite extraordinarily incompetent leadership which was to characterise the employment of their surface forces throughout the South Atlantic campaign. When further details are revealed one may have to revise this view; but if the foray by the carrier, the cruiser, and most of the ANA's escorts was not determined enough to survive a single loss to an RN submarine, it is hard to understand what this apparently major operation could have hoped to achieve in the first place. The most logical employment for the *General Belgrano* would have been as a floating battery in Stanley harbour, where her guns and missiles would have been a useful asset for the defenders. They could have continued to be fought even if she had been sunk in the shallow waters of the harbour. The Argentine Navy had had a full month in which to sail her to Stanley before the arrival of the Task Force, one of many opportunities which they neglected.

The *Belgrano* was not to be the only Argentine loss on 2 May. Later that day two 'Z-28' Type patrol craft of the Prefectura Naval, the *Rio Iguazú* and *Islas Malvinas*, were attacked by helicopters while searching for shot-down aircrew; the former was sunk, and the latter driven ashore and beached in a damaged but not irreparable condition. There was something prophetic in the disabling of a vessel bearing the Argentine name of the islands.

The next day, 3 May, the Argentine Navy's losing streak continued. The two armed tugs *Comodoro Somellera* and *Alférez Sobral*, which represented the permanent presence of the Argentine Navy in the Falklands, sallied forth early in the morning from Stanley to search for survivors of the patrol boats. One of them was detected by a Sea King helicopter, which radioed for reinforcements when the tug opened fire. A Lynx from HMS *Coventry*, armed with Sea Skua missiles, arrived in response, and sank the *Comodoro Somellera*. Another helicopter from *Hermes* was sent out to search for survivors, and was fired upon by *Sobral*, which was in turn attacked with Sea Skuas by a Lynx from *Glasgow*. Damaged, the *Sobral* limped into Puerto Deseado on the mainland two days later with her bridge blown away and her captain and seven other crew members dead.

On the same day it was announced that the Admiralty was requisitioning the world's largest

Pre-war shot of HMS *Antelope*, the Amazon class frigate lost on the morning of 24 May after a 500lb bomb, which lodged in the engine room during a raid on the previous day, exploded while being defused and set fire to her fuel. (MoD)

passenger liner, Cunard's *Queen Elizabeth 2*, as a transport for reinforcements for the Task Force. Also requisitioned were the car ferries *Baltic Ferry* and *Nordic Ferry*, and the container ship *Atlantic Causeway*. These vessels were to transport the men and heavy equipment of 5 Infantry Brigade, which was to serve as tactical reserve for 3 Cdo.Bde. and to garrison the Falklands after their liberation.

To minimise the effects of sending almost all of the available units of the Royal Navy to the South Atlantic, the Admiralty announced that the old carrier *Bulwark*, which had been decommissioned and awaiting scrapping at Portsmouth for over a year, was to be re-activated. The same decision was reached over the frigates *Gurkha*, *Tartar* and *Zulu*, which had been earmarked for sale to Venezuela, and the 'Rothesay' Class frigate *Berwick*, which was also on the disposal list.

The following day it was the turn of the Task Force to suffer substantial losses. On the morning of 4 May a Sea Harrier from No.809 NAS on *Hermes* was shot down by ground fire while on a bombing

Sea Dart area air defence missile being fired from HMS *Bristol*; **during Operation 'Corporate' the Sea Dart was credited with eight enemy aircraft. (MoD)**

mission over Goose Green, and its pilot killed. Several hours later, in the early afternoon, while on radar picket duty west of the Falklands, the Type 42 destroyer HMS *Sheffield* was attacked by three Super Etendard aircraft of the Argentine Navy's 2nd Fighter/Attack Squadron. Two AM.39 Exocet air-to-surface missiles were launched; one was apparently deflected by CORVUS chaff fired from the *Sheffield*'s dispenser but the second struck her between the operations room and forward machinery room, and although the warhead failed to explode the impact and the residual fuel caused immediate and serious fires.

The details of this incident are, naturally enough, classified under the terms of the Official Secrets Act. There is considerable speculation about the radar systems on *Sheffield*, and the manner in which they were used, but without an authorative report there seems little point in repeating guesswork. The Type 965 aerial apparently continued to rotate up to the moment of impact, but the set's status at that moment is not known; SCOT communications gear

was in use, and may have interfered with the EW set. The ship was not at 'full', only 'second degree' alert; thus some crew did not have anti-flash gear on. The missile was sighted from the bridge some 20 seconds before impact, and was not spotted by EW.

Apart from the rapidly-spreading fire, *Sheffield* suffered a loss of power which greatly hindered damage control attempts. After a four-hour fight against the flames her commanding officer, Capt. James Salt, ordered her abandoned. Enemy submarines were active in the vicinity—a torpedo was definitely fired, and detected by British sonar—and Capt. Salt considered that the futile efforts to save his ship were distracting and endangering other Task Force vessels. (The frigate *Arrow* was laid close alongside the *Sheffield* in an effort to assist her, and in great and obvious danger.) Of *Sheffield*'s crew of 270, 20 men died and 24 others were seriously injured. The survivors were transferred to other ships of the Task Force for passage to *Hermes*.

It seems probable that both of the Argentine Type 209 submarines were in the vicinity. Some reason exists to believe that one of them may have been hit, and perhaps sunk, by a Stingray torpedo released from a Sea King helicopter. Details of this action, too, are at present classified.

The loss of the *Sheffield* seemed to 'even things up' for the sinking of the *General Belgrano*, and international opinion began to swing back to some extent behind Britain. Surprisingly to some observers, this first major loss of British lives did not appreciably weaken British public support for the 'military option' adopted by Mrs. Thatcher's government. The mood became grimmer, but no less determined. Voices were raised on the far Right of the political spectrum demanding the (militarily attractive but diplomatically disastrous) bombing of the mainland Argentine air bases; and on the far Left, demanding the retreat of the Task Force. Neither attracted significant support.

The next four days were relatively quiet, although two further Sea Harriers—from No.801 NAS, on *Invincible*—were lost in an obscure flying accident in atrocious weather. A batch of replacements, fitted for air-to-air refuelling, performed a record nine-hour flight non-stop from Britain to Ascension; most of them—a mixture of Sea Harriers and RAF GR.3 types—were loaded aboard *Atlantic Conveyor* for the last leg, but three

THE COLOUR PLATES

Credits:
Front cover—BBC TV News.
Plates A top, A bottom left, D bottom, G top, and H—all Paul Haley, 'Soldier' Magazine.
Plates A bottom right, B, C, D top, E, F, and G bottom—all taken by naval photographers serving aboard HM ships, and released through Fleet Photographic Unit, HMS *Excellent*, Portsmouth.

Front cover

Sea Harrier FRS.1 V/STOL jet fighter-bombers of Nos.800 and 899 Naval Air Squadrons on the flight deck of HMS *Hermes* in rough weather—note the wave breaking over the 'ski-jump' ramp high on the carrier's bow. The fighters carry 100gal. drop-tanks on the inboard wing pylons and AIM-9L Sidewinder air-to-air missiles outboard. They are painted glossy dark sea grey all over, with low-visibility blue and red roundels on intakes and upper wings; normal ejection, rescue, and 'keep off' stencils are retained.

A top

Troops of 5 Infantry Brigade—some with blue civilian rucksacks, a reminder of the haste with which the Task Force was kitted out for South Atlantic winter warfare—practice emplaning on Sea King helicopters of No.825 NAS on the rapidly-fitted rear helicopter deck of *Queen Elizabeth 2*. The sunshine indicates that this was taken relatively early in the voyage—in fact, off Sierra Leone.

A bottom left

Two cold soldiers man a GPMG lashed to the rail of *Canberra*. The improvised light anti-aircraft batteries of dozens of GPMGs, M2 Brownings and Bren LMGs lashed all over the warships and transports proved extremely effective when heavy enemy air attacks became a daily feature of life in San Carlos Water.

A bottom right

The helicopters lifted everything—including other helicopters! Here 'Bravo Uncle', a Chinook HC.1 of No. 18 Sqn. RAF, lifts a storm-damaged Wessex from the rear deck of HMS *Glamorgan*. It was 'Bravo November' of this squadron which achieved miracles of endurance, and lift figures beyond the designers' nightmares, when the loss of *Atlantic Conveyor* left it the only surviving Chinook.

B top

HMS *Antrim*, D18, anchored off South Georgia. It was *Antrim*'s Wessex helicopter which extracted the SAS recce party, and the crews of the two helicopters which had already crashed in earlier attempts, off the Fortuna Glacier under blizzard conditions. *Antrim* gave close NGS for the recapture of the island, and her helicopter dropped the depth charges which crippled the enemy submarine *Santa Fé*.

B bottom

Argentine aircraft hit *Antrim* hard while she was covering the landings at San Carlos on 21 May; two 1,000lb. bombs penetrated her hull but failed to explode, and she was strafed with cannon fire. Above the cannon holes may be seen a Sea Cat SAM launcher, and the busy helicopter hangar—like several warships, *Antrim* handled far more than her official capacity of helicopters during the campaign.

C top

A Sea King and a Wessex taking part in the constant traffic of helicopters ferrying supplies and munitions from the logistic support flotilla to the beachhead at San Carlos. In the background, the *Norland*; at right, one of the landing craft engaged in the same duty. Landing craft came from both the RM flotilla attached to the assault ships, and from the Royal Corps of Transport. Some were camouflaged white and dark sea grey, others white and light blue, and the RCT vessels drab green and black.

C bottom

The crew take to the raft from a ditched Sea King, kept afloat by air bags on a relatively calm day. The fate of helicopter crews who ditched at night or in gale conditions was far more questionable.

D top

HMS *Fearless* under attack from Argentine Dagger fighter-bombers in 'Bomb Alley' during the San Carlos landings. At least 14 enemy Daggers, Mirages and Skyhawks were shot down over the beachhead on 21 May.

D bottom

A wickedly clear day in 'Bomb Alley' . . . the work of unloading goes on without rest, seen here from the door-gunner's perch of a Sea King helicopter.

E top

The death of a frigate: HMS *Antelope*, F170, breaks her back and sinks in San Carlos Water on 24 May, the morning after the explosion of an enemy bomb during attempts to defuse it started uncontrollable fires on the already damaged warship.

E bottom

The death of a destroyer: HMS *Coventry*, D118, rolls over with most of her port side blown away, 26 May. After taking a heavy toll of enemy aircraft she was caught by two pairs of Skyhawks which came in from port and starboard almost simultaneously during the 20-second 'warm-up' period during which her Sea Darts could not be launched.

F top

HMS *Plymouth*, F126, burns in Falkland Sound on 8 June, with HMS *Avenger*, F185, in attendance. One of the Dagger jets which did the damage was brought down with Sea Cat SAMs, and the fire was successfully controlled, with only five men wounded.

A

B

D

F

H

may have flown on direct to the carriers by means of further in-flight refuelling rendezvous. Five additional destroyers and frigates also arrived, bringing the total number of escort vessels to about two dozen.

On 7 May the TEZ was extended to within 12 miles of the Argentine coast; on the 11th Argentina retaliated by declaring their own, overlapping exclusion zone, but their fear of British submarines rendered this rather a hollow gesture.

Throughout 9 and 10 May Task Force ships bombarded shore installations on the islands, including Stanley airport, while Harriers carried out repeated low-level raids. In the early morning of the 9th two Harriers intercepted and shot up the Argentine trawler *Narwal*, suspected of spying on the Task Force; her crew of 26 lost one dead and 14 wounded, and the survivors were taken off by Sea King. *Narwal* was boarded, and she and *Sheffield*—miraculously, still afloat—were taken in tow; but the destroyer finally sank when the weather worsened the following day.

Despite the TEZ Argentine supply ships, displaying rather more spirit than their Navy's combat vessels, continued to run the blockade. On 11 May HMS *Alacrity*, probing by night the waters of Falkland Sound, which divides East from West Falkland, surprised and sank by gunfire the *Isla de Los Estados* during the course of a mission to reconnoitre enemy positions and to test the Sound's navigability by major warships.

On 12 May—the day on which *QE2* sailed from Southampton with the Scots and Welsh Guards and Gurkha Rifles of 5 Inf.Bde.—Argentine air attacks resumed with renewed fury. Successive waves of Skyhawks escorted by Mirage fighters attacked the destroyers *Broadsword* and *Glasgow* about 25 miles east of Stanley; they had been bombarding Argentine shore positions on East Falkland. The first wave was broken up by Sea Wolf missiles, and two Skyhawks were claimed by *Broadsword*; but an A-4P in the second wave managed to hit *Glasgow* with a 1,000lb. bomb. It passed straight through her without exploding, causing damage which cost her power for several hours. Later that day a Sea King was forced to ditch, although fortunately its crew were picked up without injury.

British air operations resumed on 14 May, and on the night of 14th/15th 45 men of 22 SAS Regt. and a small naval artillery observation and communications unit from *Hermes* landed from three helicopters on Pebble Island. With gunfire support from HMS *Glamorgan*, they carried out a daring raid on the air strip, destroying 11 aircraft including six Pucarás and—the priority target—radar installations which could have given warning of the forthcoming landings at San Carlos; they also inflicted casualties, and withdrew with only two slightly wounded.

On 16 May Harriers from *Hermes* on Combat Air Patrol spotted and sank an Argentine supply vessel

---

THE COLOUR PLATES (Cont.)

F bottom
Damage control crews at work on HMS *Glamorgan*, D19, after she was hit by a shore-launched Exocet missile from enemy positions in Stanley on 11 June. The missile detonated in mid-air thanks to effective countermeasures, thus limiting damage and casualties.

G top
Two days after the disastrous air attack at Fitzroy, *Sir Galahad* still burns steadily. She was later towed out and scuttled, being dedicated as a war grave for the 48 men who died aboard.

G bottom
Inspection of damage aboard the *Sir Tristram*, with the burning *Sir Galahad* in the background. The two logistic landing ships were hit on 8 June while disembarking 1st Bn. The Welsh Guards in daylight

and before the Rapier SAM batteries landed earlier could be fully set up for action.

H top
Crowded with Harriers and helicopters, streaked with rust and marked by the sea, HMS *Hermes* was still on full alert when this photograph was taken somewhere in the TEZ' shortly after the collapse of enemy resistance on the islands.

H bottom
The Argentine patrol craft *Islas Malvinas*, shot up by British helicopters on 2 May but later repaired, was captured intact in Stanley harbour: note the three-tone camouflage scheme. This 'Z-28' Class boat was promptly taken over as a prize and pressed into service, being crewed by men from HMS *Cardiff*; in honour of the famously boisterous seamen's quarter of that city, it was rechristened 'HMS *Tiger Bay*'!

at the southern end of Falkland Sound, and exchanged fire with the transport *Bahia Buen Suceso* while it lay at anchor off Fox Bay on West Falkland.

The failure of UN Secretary General Pérez de Cuéllar's last-ditch diplomatic attempts to find a solution to the confrontation led on 20 May to the Task Force being placed on 'Red Alert'. After more than six weeks at sea it was becoming obvious that the time was approaching when the combat readiness of the embarked troops would begin to decline. If a landing were to be made on the Falklands, it has to come within a matter of days.

Return to the Falklands

Preparations for a landing had been in train since it became clear that the Secretary General's mediation would come to nothing. The Harrier reinforcements were transhipped from *Atlantic Conveyor* to the two carriers in preparation for intensive operations. Troops began to transfer to assault craft from the transports in which they had travelled the 8,000 miles from the United Kingdom. During this phase 21 men—19 of them from 22 SAS Regt.—were lost in a helicopter accident apparently caused by bird-strike in appalling conditions of darkness and bad weather.

Following the Pebble Island raid the Argentines had been encouraged to think that further British

HMS *Onyx*, flying the Jolly Roger on her return to the UK, is the only conventionally powered submarine known to have taken part in 'Corporate'. She carried out a number of clandestine missions, and one source states with confidence that she landed SBS/SAS parties on the mainland to observe Argentine bases, and to attack the airfield at Rio Gallegos. (Whether this attack ever took place is still unconfirmed.) During this landing mission *Onyx* ran aground on an uncharted reef and damaged her hull and torpedo tubes, causing a live torpedo to become jammed in the tube. (Mike Lennon)

raids would take place, as part of the softening-up process, before a landing in force was eventually made—probably on relatively lightly-held West Falkland. While creating this impression by means of noisy hit-and-run raids by special forces, Adm. Woodward and ground force commander Maj.Gen. Jeremy Moore were planning something considerably more enterprising. It had been decided that a major landing would be made at San Carlos Bay on the west coast of East Falkland. The proposed site had several attractive advantages. It faced Falkland Sound, which gave a measure of protection from airborne attack, as the enemy 'planes would have only a limited run-in before launching their ordnance. The bay was surrounded by hills, which would form a useful defensive perimeter once the beachhead was established. Finally and most surprisingly, the area was only weakly garrisoned by an understrength company of infantry—and this despite a detailed Argentine intelligence appreciation which had identified it as one of the most likely beachheads.

On the night of 20 May the Task Force split into two major elements; the larger, containing the assault ships and transports, sailed along the north coast of East Falkland towards the designated landing area, while the carriers and their defensive screens proceeded in a south-westerly direction. Smaller detachments of two or three destroyers and frigates bombarded Stanley and Port Louis, while the Harriers carried out bombing raids on Stanley, Goose Green and Fox Bay, and landing parties at all of these points created considerable confusion among the enemy.

At dawn on 21 May, screened by the destroyer

HMS *Antrim* and four frigates, the troops of 3 Commando Brigade went ashore at San Carlos from the troopship *Canberra* and the assault ships *Fearless* and *Intrepid*, meeting only weak resistance. The Argentines fell back, leaving nine wounded prisoners, after shooting down two Royal Marine Gazelle helicopters—possibly, with British-manufactured Blowpipe missiles.

The first reaction came in the form of air strikes by the Pucarás based at Stanley and Goose Green, and the MB.339s from Stanley. Two or three Pucarás were shot down without causing serious damage. More formidable opposition developed in mid-morning when 16 A-4s escorted by Mirage fighters attacked the landing flotilla in waves of four. Two 1,000lb. bombs hit the *Antrim* in the engine room, failing to explode and later being defused by bomb disposal experts. The frigate *Ardent*, which was bombarding Goose Green, was not so lucky. She was hit by two 500lb. bombs and 14 ballistic rockets fired by the Aermacchi MB.339As of the Argentine Navy's 1st Attack Sqn. from Stanley, and burst into flames at once; she sank several hours later, losing 24 dead and 30 wounded from her crew of 170.

The air attacks continued throughout the hours of daylight; the Argentines are believed to have lost a total of 14 Mirages, Daggers and Skyhawks, and one Harrier of No.1 Sqn. RAF was shot down by a Blowpipe missile. By nightfall some 5,000 British troops were ashore in a secure beachhead some ten square miles in area—and another four Task Force ships had suffered damage.

The following day the landing forces enjoyed a respite as the FAA regrouped; two Skyhawks which ventured towards the ships veered off at the approach of the Sea Harrier CAP. Consolidation of the beachhead continued, as did bombardment of enemy shore positions. The Argentine merchant fleet continued to put their Navy to shame by bravely running the blockade, and the freighter *Monsunan* was driven ashore in Choiseul Sound after being strafed by two Sea Harriers.

On the 23rd the Argentine air forces returned to the attack with a vengeance. Varying their tactics, successive pairs of Mirages, Skyhawks and Daggers attacked the ships and the troops ashore; the latter had now set up Rapier SAM batteries, which took a toll of the attackers. Five Mirages and/or Daggers

The missile launcher and tracking radar of the Sea Wolf SAM system; and the manual loading of the launcher. This short-range anti-missile and anti-aircraft defence system uses line-of-sight guidance by radar or TV camera. Sea Wolf is usually fired in salvoes of two, to maximise kill probability; it is credited with five enemy aircraft in the Falklands campaign. The extremely manoeuvrable missile has a speed above Mach 2, and TV tracking is used for low-level targets. (MoD)

and one A-4 were confirmed as destroyed. Nevertheless, the Royal Navy was to suffer yet another loss when two 500lb. bombs dropped by a Skyhawk at masthead height struck the frigate HMS *Antelope*. The Skyhawk was destroyed by a missile seconds later; but the bombs avenged the pilot some hours after his death. One started a fire, which was being brought under control while a bomb disposal expert, Staff Sergeant Jim Prescott, worked on the other. It seems that in his haste an Argentine armourer had inserted the fuse the wrong way round; this departure from normal configuration misled Prescott, and the bomb

HMS *Hermes*, flagship of the Task Force, on her return to the UK. On deck can be seen various aircraft which took part in 'Corporate'. Forard are six Sea Harriers, and six Sea King HAS.5 ASW helicopters of No.826 NAS; at positions 3 and 4 are two RAF Pumas; at 5 and 6 are two more HAS.5 Sea Kings, and a Commando Sea King HC.4 of No.846; and right aft are an HAS.5 and an HC.4, four Wessex and two Lynx. (C. S. Taylor)

detonated under his hands, killing him instantly. The fire then spread and became uncontrollable; and the explosion of *Antelope* against the night sky provided the world with a sobering and unforgettable news picture. The aluminium superstructure of the frigate collapsed in the intense heat, and the crew were forced to abandon ship; a second man had died before she sank the following day, and seven were wounded in this, the third major RN warship loss of the campaign. During this same raid *Glasgow* suffered slight damage from a 1,000lb. bomb which passed through her plates without exploding.

Further air attacks followed on 24 May; two RFA supply ships were damaged, for the loss of six Mirages or Daggers and two A-4s. With most of their supplies now ashore, the troops began to broaden the perimeter of the beachhead; bombardment of enemy shore positions continued meanwhile. A Harrier was lost in a take-off accident.

It had been expected that the Argentines would make a supreme effort on 25 May, their Independence Day; and they did. Reverting to the tactic of sending in flights of four aircraft, successive waves of Skyhawks struck at three radar picket ships deployed north-west of the beachhead, in an attempt to take advantage of the Task Force's critical lack of an airborne early warning capability. The *Argonaut* was hit by two bombs which failed to explode; the damage they caused was severe enough to keep her in dockyard hands for nearly a year when she returns home, however. *Broadsword* was also struck by a bomb which failed to explode but which destroyed her helicopter and badly damaged her hangar. The *Coventry* was not so lucky.

Having already downed one Skyhawk reconnaissance aircraft with a Sea Dart SAM, and no less than four others with further missiles and gunfire, the *Coventry* was preparing to launch further Sea Darts when the second wave of A-4s hit her. Two came in very low over the starboard side, followed by a second pair from port. The gyros on the booster motors of the Sea Darts require 20 seconds to warm up after being lifted from the cooled magazine; and it was during this period that the second wave of Skyhawks struck, while the ship was without missile defence. Her port side half blown away, *Coventry* rolled over to port; she was abandoned with the loss of 17 men.

Later that day two Super Etendards of the Argentine Navy's 2nd Fighter/Attack Squadron, now flying from Rio Gallegos, fired AM.39 Exocet ASMs at ships of the Task Force. One struck the 15,000-ton container ship *Atlantic Conveyor* as she made her way round the north-eastern tip of East Falkland. At the time of the attack, which was carried out at the extremely close range of four to six miles, the aircraft's intended target was HMS *Hermes*. The first Exocet was deflected off course by means of a Sea King flying as a decoy. Unfortunately its homing head then picked up another large target—*Atlantic Conveyor*. The missile struck near the stern, and exploded. A great sheet of

Armourers moving weapons to re-arm helicopters for an ASW mission from *Hermes* off the Falklands. All wear anti-flash gear, and carry their respirators slung at the waist. The weapon at left is a Mk 11 depth charge, that on the right a Mk 46 torpedo. (Martin Cleaver, Press Association)

flame spread forwards between decks the full length of the vessel, and the ship had to be abandoned. Her loss was a severe blow to the Task Force; although the Harriers had been flown to the carriers and ashore, she was still carrying much heavy equipment for the troops, and in particular four Chinook heavy-lift helicopters and 15 Wessex, vital for the planned advance across the island. Only one Chinook, apparently aloft on an air test, survived the raid. On the container ship Capt. Ian North and 11 members of his crew died; blackened and burnt out, she remained afloat for some days. The second Exocet fired in this incident was also successfully decoyed from *Hermes* by chaff and other ECM devices.

The following day there was no enemy air activity, but the Harriers hit Stanley yet again. On the 27th the Argentines returned to the attack, striking at ground targets rather than the ships off shore. The main focus of operations was now ashore, as the Royal Marines and Paras moved out

Sea King HAS.5 of No.826 Sqn from *Hermes*—the Magnetic Anomaly Detection gear can be seen under the starboard float. The RN's Sea King 5s use sonobuoys to detect submarines; set patterns are laid, and the buoys 'listen' for submarine noises and radio them to the helicopter. The signals are electronically processed and the results displayed on a screen; an arithmetical solution indicates the probable course of the submarine, which is tracked using further sonobuoys while the MAD equipment—which detects minute changes in the Earth's magnetic field—is used to further localise the target's position. The target is then attacked using a homing torpedo. (Paul Beaver)

A rather more direct method of hitting the enemy is employed by a Commando Sea King HC.4 of No.846 Sqn operating from HMS *Hermes*—a twin GPMG mount in the door, operated by Sgt. Hannah RM with RN CPO Aircrewman Kelly as loader. Many Commando helicopters were fitted with door guns for self-defence against ground fire, and to give support to troops. (MoD)

of the beachhead in two directions: eastwards across the island towards Stanley, and southwards towards Goose Green and Darwin. On 28 May 2nd Bn. The Parachute Regt. captured Goose Green in fierce fighting against odds of more than two to one. The settlements of Douglas and Teal Inlet on the north coast were also recaptured by advancing Royal Marines. During the following two days frigates once more bombarded Stanley, in concert with Harrier raids. The men of 5 Inf.Bde., transhipped from *QE2* at South Georgia, now landed at San Carlos, almost doubling the available British land forces. The Argentine garrison, although still much stronger than the landing forces, was now largely bottled up around Stanley, abandoning the initiative to Gen. Moore. The noose was tightening.

It would appear from persistent Argentine reports that there was a further Exocet attack on 30 May; British sources are unforthcoming, beyond confirming that an Exocet was released. A pair of

Etendards escorted by four Skyhawks from IV Brigada Aerea apparently took part, and later claimed to have sunk or disabled HMS *Invincible* for the loss of two A-4s. The survivors reported heavy smoke rising from the target ship; *Invincible* was certainly not hit on the 30th, or any other day, and it is now generally accepted that the target was the hulk of *Atlantic Conveyor*, deliberately towed into position as a decoy. HMS *Avenger* later claimed to have destroyed an Exocet with a lucky shot from her 4.5in gun on this date.

Throughout the next week the land forces and their supporting aircraft had a monopoly of action as they 'yomped' towards Stanley. Sea transport carried a force round the coast to outflank the capital from the south; in a daring heli-borne coup a company of Paras leap-frogged forward to seize Bluff Cove, a just-abandoned settlement on the coast about 10 miles south-west of Stanley, and the following morning—6 June—2nd Bn. The Scots Guards reinforcements arrived aboard *Intrepid*. Bad weather delayed the arrival of 1st Bn. The Welsh Guards aboard *Sir Tristram* and *Sir Galahad* at nearby Fitzroy until 8 June. There was further delay in unloading the troops, as the Rapier SAM batteries required time to set up after their rough handling, and were given priority; this meant that troops were still being landed in daylight. Early that afternoon two Argentine Daggers and two Skyhawks came 'hedgehopping' down an inland valley to hit the two landing ships with devastating effect from masthead height. *Sir Tristram* was badly damaged, and two crew were killed. On *Sir Galahad*, which was set ablaze at once, three officers and two men of the crew and 43 Welsh Guardsmen and Sappers were killed; 11 crew and 46 soldiers were wounded, many of them severely. At sunset five Skyhawks attacked the survivors on the beach, but four were claimed shot down by the missile batteries and automatic weapons now established on the

The converted container ship *Atlantic Conveyor*: the open 'hangar' made of cargo containers shelters two RAF Chinooks and three Wessex helicopters, as well as fuel cells. A Sea Harrier FRS.1 of No.809 NAS—commissioned on 6 April—prepares to land on the marked area visible forard. (MoD)

high ground. There is still much speculation about the reasons for Argentine success in this raid; one factor was the failure of an RAF Vulcan mission from Ascension on 31 May to destroy completely the enemy's 3-D surveillance radar on Two Sisters mountain. Three of four Shrike missiles were released, one 'hanging up'; one landed yards from the radar and knocked the antenna over, but in the next few days the Argentines managed to repair it in time to witness the Fitzroy landing.

Air attacks also took place against HMS *Fearless* in Choiseul Sound, during which landing craft 'F4' was sunk with the loss of six men. The frigate *Plymouth* was also hit by Daggers and Skyhawks while patrolling at the north end of Falkland Sound; five of her crew were wounded, but she was able to control the damage, and shot down a Dagger with Sea Cat missiles.

With this last effort, the Argentine air forces appeared to have shot their bolt. No further significant air attacks were made against the Task Force. The Royal Navy still had to suffer its last casualties, however: on the night of 11 June HMS *Glamorgan* was hit by a land-launched Exocet while bombarding shore positions at Stanley. The missile passed across the port side of the destroyer's flight deck and detonated in mid-air, which saved *Glamorgan* from crippling damage. Nevertheless, fires were started; the hangar was badly damaged, the Wessex helicopter destroyed, 13 men killed and another 17 wounded.

Three days later it was all over. At one minute to midnight GMT on Monday 14 June Gen. Menéndez surrendered all Argentine troops on the Falklands to Gen. Moore. The Falklands War had lasted 74 days, and had cost the lives of 255 British and more than 1,000 Argentine service personnel.

31

Summary and Conclusions

The Falklands War was the first major amphibious campaign to be fought in the past 25 years. The feat of mounting it, at a distance of more than 4,000 miles from the nearest friendly base, was both spectacular, and without parallel in modern history. The British forces—land, sea and air—won so devastatingly because, quite simply, they were better trained, better motivated and better led.

Argentine propaganda made much of the supposed ignorance of British 'mercenaries' of the cause for which they were fighting. It is surprising that their enemies should find it so hard to understand that simple identification with the homely, familiar, and frightened faces of the islanders staring from their newspapers and TV screens provided British servicemen with the most powerful motivation of all. To sophisticated Argentine commentators British insistence on protecting the liberties of 1,800 countrymen seems, even now, impossibly 'romantic'. To British public opinion it was the most basic requirement of self-respect. At the necessarily more cynical level of political life, any British voter could have told the Junta that no Conservative Party government could survive for as much as a week a failure to fight in such a cause.

The fact remains that Britain was extremely lucky. In order to win she was forced to mobilise almost her entire naval forces, and to impress a very sizeable portion of her merchant fleet, stripping her naval commitment to NATO to the bone in the process. Had the Junta waited only a few months until the Nott defence cuts had really started to take effect, Britain would not have had the military ability to mount the Task Force, nor the amphibious assault capability to re-invade the islands. As it was, Adm. Woodward freely admitted that had one of his two carriers been sunk or put out of action the Task Force would have had to withdraw. Had the Argentine Navy displayed more enterprise it might well have accomplished this.

The poor performance of Adm. Anaya's navy is surprising, given its position, for so long, as the premier navy in Latin America. Its sole carrier is reported to have suffered from machinery trouble for most of the campaign; thus its failure to leave harbour after the foray at the beginning of May is rationalised. It seems equally likely that the fate of the *Belgrano* had such a traumatic effect that Anaya baulked at the prospect of losing his major status symbol by exposing it to battle—a classic confusion of symbolism with the real power which it is supposed to represent.

The *General Belgrano* itself, even allowing for its limited military potential, was totally misused and needlessly sacrificed, along with more than 300 lives. One of the Type 42 destroyers is reported to have been damaged by grounding at some stage of the campaign. The corvette damaged in the invasion of South Georgia spent most of the campaign in dry dock.

Although the two Type 209 submarines were reported to have been present when HMS *Sheffield* was disabled, the Argentine submarine arm also seems to have achieved remarkably little. The British troopships presented a tempting target on the long voyage south, and it was fear of submarines which kept the *QE2*, in particular, out of the war zone, transferring her troops at South Georgia. The Argentines themselves do not seem to have envisaged the employment of their submarines in their classic role. The use of *Santa Fé* as a supply and troop transport was an obvious example of the

The *Atlantic Conveyor* **still burning hours after being hit by an Exocet on 25 May. The Harriers had already transferred to** *Hermes* **and** *Invincible*, **but only one Chinook survived of the helicopters. The burnt-out hulk of a Wessex can just be seen between the foremost containers, and the remains of a Chinook on the stern. (MoD)**

The assault ship HMS *Fearless*, showing the effects of continuous operations in the South Atlantic. She survived repeated air attacks at San Carlos. The home of No.846 helicopter squadron during the landings, she achieved well in excess of 4,000 deck landings during 'Corporate', including Sea Harriers on occasion. (C. & S. Taylor)

An LCM.9 from HMS *Fearless*, finished in dark blue-grey and white, with the four Scimitar and two Scorpion light AFVs of the Blues and Royals which fought in the Falklands. The troops hit the beaches at San Carlos at 0400hrs on 21 May, not much more than a thousand hours after the Argentine invasion of Stanley. The enemy air attacks which followed concentrated on warships rather than the vulnerable and more immediately vital transports—a fatal mistake. For the initial landings the AFVs—presumably dispersed between several LCMs—were ashore early to provide direct support for the infantry. (C. & S. Taylor)

misuse of submarines, the folly of which had been amply demonstrated by the Japanese in the Second World War.

In contrast with the incompetent leadership and poor performance of the surface forces, the fighter-bomber pilots, though not the interceptors, were generally both brave and skilful, exciting the admiration of their enemies. They hit approximately 75 per cent of the surface warships of the Task Force, sinking or totally disabling two destroyers, two frigates, two logistic landing ships and a container ship. The failure of many of their

A Sea Harrier lands on the deck of *Fearless* to refuel, as early morning sun casts long shadows in San Carlos Water. The versatility of the aircraft is such that it can operate from virtually any platform where there is space for it to land, and strength to bear its weight and the heat of its engine. Background, the LSL *Sir Percival* and the ferry *Elk* (right); *Elk* had a makeshift hangar under the white bow structure and a landing deck aft of it. (MoD)

Two of the damage control team on *Invincible* check their fire-fighting suits and breathing apparatus, ready for action. The fire and smoke hazard was shown to be a major contributory cause to ship losses suffered by the Task Force. Toxic fumes given off by plastic materials used for furnishings and wall coverings sometimes prevented teams from reaching the real seat of the fire. (MoD)

bombs to detonate was an obvious curiosity of the campaign. The bombs were designed for use against land and armoured targets, and used delayed action fuses. They did not become armed until after falling for a set number of revolutions of the propeller in the arming device. The low level from which they were in most cases released did not allow this to happen; and the thin plating of modern warships allowed them to pass right through without detonating from impact. (To suggest, as some commentators have, that this was undeserved luck for the Task Force is hardly just: it was the Task Force which created the conditions which forced the pilots to fly at very low level if they hoped to survive.)

The war was interesting as a major testing-ground for modern weaponry. Although the true facts will be slow to emerge into public scrutiny, we may make some informed assumptions.

Although the effects of the French Exocet were deadly enough, it is interesting to note that of the missiles currently known to have been launched two failed to detonate; one did explode; and one and possibly two were decoyed from their targets by an effective combination of Sea King helicopters simulating a target with ECM, and ship-borne active ECM using CORVUS-launched chaff

rockets. Security currently prevents the examination of reasons why two of the Exocets failed to detonate. Nevertheless, as they had been launched well within their range parameters the unspent fuel did in fact cause serious fires in the vessels they struck. This was especially the case in HMS *Sheffield*, where the burning fuel and the internal damage caused by impact ignited the ship's fuel from a ruptured pipeline. This set fire to plastic-covered cabling, which gave off thick, black, toxic fumes in such quantities that damage control parties were effectively blinded within a very few moments. The fire main was also ruptured, and pumping machinery destroyed, which ultimately forced the crew to abandon ship.

The campaign has shown British warships to be well constructed and with a high degree of integrity, able to absorb a tremendous amount of punishment. The main fault lies in some of the materials used. The light aluminium alloy used in superstructure has a low melting point, which leads to severe problems of damage control and fire containment. Toxic fumes from PVC-covered cables and foam-filled internal furnishings also proved a major hazard for the crews (while the use of man-made materials in combat uniforms exacerbated burn injuries). The provision and powering of fire-fighting equipment also caused problems. In the case of the *Sheffield*, which relied on a single main, the destruction of pipes in this main and pump damage led ultimately to her loss.

The Type 42 'Sheffield' Class had 40ft of their length cut off in the design stage; this limited her AA defence to one SAM launcher forward, leaving a blind arc aft, and gave insufficient room for the later fitting of the Sea Wolf system.

The performance of Sea Wolf has been said to have been disappointing. This is a dubious statement to make before all the records have been assessed; and current estimates give it a 'kill' record of five aircraft. However, certain factors are worth noting. One relates to the guidance system, particularly the tracking radar. This has been shown to have difficulty in tracking targets at low level, particularly surface-skimming missiles, which it can fail to separate from the 'sea clutter'—the background returns of the sea. In its present form Sea Wolf is thus unable to deal, in many circumstances, with very low-flying targets. A

lightweight version will become available next year, but its entry into fleet service has been delayed by various political and industrial machinations.

The limitations of Sea Dart are discussed in the paragraph on the loss of HMS *Coventry*; apart from this delay before firing, Sea Dart does seem to have achieved a reasonable degree of success, and is tentatively credited with eight enemy aircraft. Sea Cat, although generally regarded as obsolete since it is a first-generation SAM with a manual optical guidance system using radio commands, has nevertheless achieved a number of successes; both *Plymouth* and *Fearless* brought down attacking jets with Sea Cat, and it is believed to have destroyed a total of eight aircraft.

Such was the lack of adequate close-in AA defence that any suitable weapon was mounted in any suitable position on the ships; these usually comprised the GPMGs and .50cal. Brownings of the embarked troops, which were used with considerable effect against low targets, achieving several 'kills' and, by putting up a tracer curtain over the anchorages, usefully distracting the attacking pilots. The war has certainly shown that the gun is still an essential weapon for virtually all warships. The automatic 4.5in. guns of the escort ships performed outstanding service in the bombardment role, and proved that Naval Gunfire

The County class destroyer HMS *Glamorgan* displays the damage caused by the land-launched Exocet which struck her on the night of 11/12 June (large dark tarpaulin, aft of nearer funnel). The ship took evasive action and fired Sea Cat missiles, but the Exocet exploded over the deck, destroying the hangar. Continually in action during the campaign, *Glamorgan* fired over 1,200 rounds from her 4.5in guns. (MoD)

Ships of the Task Force in line ahead, after the surrender of the enemy garrison. Leading is the Leander Group III frigate HMS *Andromeda*, **followed by** *Bristol*, *Invincible*, **a Type 22 frigate, an Amazon class frigate, RFAs, and in the far distance HMS** *Hermes*. **(MoD)**

Support is not the quaint historical survival believed by some.

The need for effective light AA guns has been realised, and vessels now sailing for the South Atlantic are being fitted with British twin 30mm and other 20mm weapons. At the height of the campaign a number of the American Vulcan/Phalanx systems were obtained as a stop-gap measure to cover the anti-missile gap; however, the Royal Navy does not at present wish to embark on wholesale acquisition of this system (which did not arrive in time to see action), and prefers to await the outcome of its investigation into a number of gun close-in weapon systems.

In judging the effectiveness of any weapons system it must be remembered that it is not simply a case of the number of shots fired and the targets hit. Many other factors are involved, such as range of detection, range when fire opened, weather conditions, radar target area, ECMs operative, etc.

On the radar side the British undoubtedly suffered from the limitations of current systems. On earlier ships of the 'Sheffield' Class the double-bedstead AKE, designed in the 1950s, was not stabilised, and lacked other refinements such as moving target indicator (MTI) which have since become available. Later ships of this class have newer, stabilised radar, but still lack MTI; an MTI retrofit capability is available, but has not been implemented on many ships for cost reasons. Finally, radar on this class has been shown to have difficulty separating low-flying targets from land masses—a limitation due to lack of MTI. Since they had identical destroyers themselves, the enemy were well aware of this.

Electronic countermeasures on British warships are also not completely effective. Most ships are fitted with Abbey Hill UUA-1 sets, which require a certain amount of manual injection, and also lack the associated jammer. Just before the Falklands crisis the Royal Navy was offered a jammer which could be automatically triggered, but for unexplained reasons turned it down.

The British nuclear powered attack submarines proved a deadly weapon, and much of the credit for the failure of the Argentine surface units to take an active part after the loss of *Belgrano* belongs to them.

While comment on the aircraft involved will mainly be found in the accompanying title MAA 135: *'Air Forces'*, it is worth noting that the Sea Harrier, despite limitations of range and, to some extent, speed, quickly achieved a position of considerable superiority over the TEZ. Likewise the helicopters, of which the Task Force had about 70, confirmed their value as ship-busters, ASW aircraft and general maids-of-all-work. The lack of AEW proved a great weakness, and was certainly responsible for at least half the British ship losses.

*   *   *

Gen. Galtieri, Adm. Anaya and Brig. Lami-Dozo embarked upon their military adventure to distract their people from their domestic problems. Instead they brought about their own political eclipse and their country's disgrace. It is ironic that, in the short term at least, such political benefit as the campaign conferred was enjoyed by the British government. It is to be hoped that the armed forces, whose professionalism and sacrifices achieved a success placed almost beyond their reach by the ill-conceived defence policies of successive governments of Britain, will reap some lasting advantage.

The frigate HMS *Phoebe* following refit and in Falklands grey colour scheme; a number of changes have already been made as a result of combat experience. Note twin 20mm Oerlikon mount on top of the bridge, replacing the MRS 3 director for the forard Sea Cat; this latter was mounted in front of the Exocets, but has also been removed. The boat davits abreast the funnel have been replaced by a Searider inflatable and crane. (C. & S. Taylor)

BELOW
HMS *Illustrious*, made ready for sea in record time, heads for the Falklands to relieve her sister-ship *Invincible*. The hard lessons taught by sea-skimming missiles have been learnt: at the aft starboard corner of the flight deck can be seen one of her two American Vulcan Phalanx Close-In Weapons System gun mounts. (C. & S. Taylor)

TECHNICAL DATA

Only names of ships which are presently believed to have sailed for or taken part in operations in the South Atlantic up to the cessation of hostilities are listed in these tables. Abbreviations used throughout are as follows:

Bldr Builder; *LD/L/C* Laid down/launched/completed; *Dp* Displacement, in standard tons, and fully loaded; *Dm* Dimensions, overall where known; *My* Machinery; *B/R* Bunkers/radius, where known; *P* Protection; *Arm* Armament, incl. embarked aircraft, normal capacity; *Ct* Complement. These details are not repeated where common to a class of vessels. (*CTL* Constructive total loss).

ROYAL NAVY

AIRCRAFT CARRIERS

Hermes/R12
Bldr Vickers *LD/L/C* 21.6.44/16.2.53/18.11.59 *Dp* 23,900 tons std., 28,700 f.l. *Dm* $744\frac{1}{4}$ oa × 90 × $28\frac{1}{2}$ ft *My* 2 shaft geared Parsons turbines, 76,000shp, 28 knots, 4 Admiralty 3-drum boilers *B* 4,200 tons furnace oil, 320 tons diesel oil *P* 1-2ins. around mags. & machinery spaces; flight deck reinforced *Arm* 2 × 4 Sea Cat SAM launcher; 5 Sea Harrier, 9 Sea King (reinforced for campaign) *Ct* 1,350

Invincible/R05
Bldr Vickers (Shipbuilding) *LD/L/C* 20.7.73/3.5.77/11.7.80 *Dp* 16,000 tons std., 19,500 f.l. *Dm* 677 oa × 90 × 24 ft *My* 4 Rolls Royce Olympus TM3B gas turbines, 112,000shp, 28 knots, 2 shafts *R* 5,000 miles at 18 knots cruising speed *Arm* 1 × 2 Sea Dart SAM launcher; 5 Sea Harriers, 9 Sea King (reinforced for campaign) *Ct* 1,000

DESTROYERS:

County Class:
Antrim/D18 — *Bldr* Fairfield SB *LD/L/C* 20.1.66/19.10.67/14.7.70
Glamorgan/D19 — *Bldr* Vickers (SB) *LD/L/C* 13.9.62/9.7.64/11.10.66
Class details: *Dp* 5,440 tons std., 6,200 f.l. *Dm* $520\frac{1}{2}$ oa × 54 × $20\frac{1}{2}$ ft *My* 2 geared steam turbines + 4 gas turbines, COSAG arrangement, 30,000 shp + 30,000shp, 30 knots, 2 shafts *Arm* 1 × 2 Sea Slug SAM launcher, 36 missiles; 4 × 1 Exocet SSM launcher; 2 × 4 Sea Cat SAM launcher; 1 × 2 4.5in. Mk 6 gun, 2 × 1 20mm Oerlikon; 1 Wessex helicopter *Ct* 472

Bristol/D23
Bldr Swan Hunter *LD/L/C* 15.11.67/30.6.69/31.3.73 *Dp* 6,100 tons std., 7,100 f.l. *Dm* 507 oa × 55 × $16\frac{3}{4}$ ft *My* 2 geared steam turbines + 2 Bristol Siddeley Marine Olympus TM1A gas turbines, COSAG arrangement, 30,000shp + 30,000shp, 28 knots, 2 shafts *R* 5,000 miles at 18 knots cruising speed *Arm* 1 × 2 Sea Dart SAM launchers, 40 missiles; 1 × 1 4.5in. Mk 8 gun, 2 × 1 20mm Oerlikon, 1 Ikara AS weapon system *Ct* 407

Sheffield Class:
Cardiff/D108 — *Bldr* Vickers (SB) *LD/L/C* 6.11.72/22.2.74/24.9.79
Coventry/D118 — *Bldr* Cammell Laird *LD/L/C* 29.1.73/21.6.74/20.10.78 **Sunk** 25.5.82
Exeter/D89 — *Bldr* Swan Hunter *LD/L/C* 22.7.76/25.4.78/19.9.80
Glasgow/D88 — *Bldr* Swan Hunter *LD/L/C* 16.4.74/14.4.76/24.5.79
Sheffield/D80 — *Bldr* Vickers (SB) *LD/L/C* 15.1.70/10.6.71/16.2.75 **Sunk** 10.5.82
Class details: *Dp* 3,500 tons std., 4,100 f.l. *Dm* 412 oa × 47 × 19 ft *My* 2 Rolls Royce Olympus TM3B gas turbines + 2 RR Tyne RM1A gas turbines, COSAG arrangement, 56,000bhp + 8,500bhp, 29 knots, 2 shafts *B/R* 600 tons/4,000 miles at 18 knots cruising speed *Arm* 1 × 2 Sea Dart SAM launcher, 24 missiles; 1 × 1 4.5in. Mk 8 gun, 2 × 1 20mm Oerlikon; 2 × 3 ASW torpedo tube; 1 Lynx helicopter *Ct* 253

FRIGATES:

Broadsword Class:
Battleaxe/F89 — *Bldr* Yarrow (SB) *LD/L/C* 4.2.76/18.5.77/28.3.80
Brilliant/F90 — *Bldr* Yarrow (SB) *LD/L/C* 25.3.77/15.12.78/15.5.81
Broadsword/F88 — *Bldr* Yarrow (SB) *LD/L/C* 7.2.75/12.5.76/3.5.79
Class details: *Dp* 3,500 tons std., 4,000 f.l. *Dm* 430 oa × $48\frac{1}{2}$ × 20 ft *My* 2 Rolls Royce Olympus TM3B gas turbines + 2 RR Tyne RM1A gas turbines, COGOG arrangement, 56,000bhp + 8,500bhp, 30 knots, 2 shafts *R* 4,500 miles at 18 knots cruising speed *Arm* 4 × 1 Exocet SSM launcher; 2 × 6 Sea Wolf SAM launcher; 2 × 1 40mm gun; 2 × 3 Mk

Electric steam turbines, 22,000shp, 21 knots, 2 shafts *B/R* 2,250 tons/5,000 miles at 20 knots *Arm* 4 × 4 Sea Cat SAM launcher; 2 × 1 40mm gun; 4 × LCVP, 4 × LCM9 in dock; 16 × 50-ton tanks + wide variety other vehicles; 700 Royal Marines for short voyage; up to 5 Wessex helicopters *Ct* 580

Logistic Landing Ships:
Sir Bedivere/L3004 — *Bldr* Hawthorn Leslie *LD/L/C* 28.10.65/20.7.66/17.5.67
Sir Galahad/L3005 — *Bldr* Stephen *LD/L/C* 22.2.65/19.4.66/17.12.66 **CTL** 8.6.82
Sir Geraint/L3027 — *Bldr* Stephen *LD/L/C* 21.2.65/26.1.67/12.7.67
Sir Lancelot/L3029 — *Bldr* Fairfield SB *LD/L/C* 29.6.62/25.6.63/18.1.64
Sir Percival/L3036 — *Bldr* Hawthorn Leslie *LD/L/C* 27.7.66/4.10.67/22.3.68
Sir Tristram/L3505 — *Bldr* Hawthorn Leslie *LD/L/C* 14.3.66/12.12.66/14.9.67 **CTL** 8.6.82
Class details: *Dp* 5,674 tons f.l. (Sir Lancelot, 5,550) *Dm* $412\frac{3}{4}$oa × 58 × $12\frac{3}{4}$ ft *My* 2 Mirlees diesel engines, 8,460bhp, 17 knots, 2 shafts (Sir Lancelot, 2 Denny Sulzer diesels, 8,250bhp) *B/R* 815 tons/8,000 miles at 15 knots (Sir Lancelot, 810 tons) *Arm* 2 × 1 40mm gun (not normally carried); 16 tanks + 34 other vehicles, 534 troops *Ct* 69

MINE WARFARE VESSELS:

Hunt Class:
Brecon/M29 — *Bldr* Vosper Thorneycroft *C* 21.3.80
Ledbury/M30 — *Bldr* Vosper Thorneycroft *C* 11.6.81
Class details: *Dp* 615 tons std, 725 f.l. *Dm* 197oa × $32\frac{3}{4}$ × $8\frac{1}{4}$ ft *My* 2 Ruston-Paxman Deltic diesels, 3,800bhp, 16 knots, 2 shafts *R* 1,500 miles at 12 knots *Arm* 1 × 1 40mm gun *Ct* 45

MISCELLANEOUS WARSHIPS:

Patrol/Despatch Vessels:
Leeds Castle/P258 — *Bldr* Hall Russell *LD/L/C* 11.79/29.10.80/27.10.81
Dumbarton Castle/P265 — *Bldr* Hall Russell *L/C* 3.6.81/1982
Class details: *Dp* 1,427 tons *Dm* $265\frac{3}{4}$ × $37\frac{3}{4}$ × 14 ft *My* 2 Ruston 12 RKCM diesels, 5,640bhp, $19\frac{1}{2}$ knots, 2 shafts *B/R* 180 tonnes/10,000 miles at 10 knots *Arm* 1 × 1 40mm gun; can land 1 Sea King helicopter *Ct* 50

Ice Patrol Ships:
Endurance/A171
Bldr Krogerwerft *LD/L/C* 1955/26.5.56/12.56 *Dp* 3,600 tons *Dm* 305 oa × 46 × $25\frac{3}{4}$ ft *My* 1 Burmeister & Wain diesel, 2,900bhp, 14 knots, 1 shaft *B/R* 545 tons/12,000 miles at 14 knots *Arm* 2 × 1 20mm; 2 Wasp helicopters *Ct* 119

HELICOPTER SUPPORT SHIPS:

Engadine/K08
Bldr Henry Robb *LD/L/C* 9.8.65/16.9.66/15.12.67 *Dp* 9,000 tons f.l. *Dm* $424\frac{1}{4}$ oa × 58 × 22 ft *My* 1 Sulzer turbocharged diesel, 5,500bhp, $14\frac{1}{2}$ knots, 1 shaft *Arm* 6 helicopters carried as required *Ct* 185

HOSPITAL SHIPS:

(converted for campaign from survey vessels; converted liners not included, e.g. Uganda)

Herald/A138
Bldr Henry Robb *LD/L/C* 9.11.72/4.10.73/31.10.74 *Dp* 2,000 tons std., 2,945 f.l. *Dm* 260 oa × 49 × $15\frac{1}{2}$ ft *My* 3 Paxman 12 YJCZ diesels, 2,434bhp, 14 knots, 1 shaft *R* 12,000 miles at 11 knots *Ct* 128. Can carry 1 Wasp helicopter

Hecla/A133 — *Bldr* Yarrow *LD/L/C* 6.5.64/21.12.64/8.9.65
Hydra/A144 — *Bldr* Yarrow *LD/L/C* 14.5.64/14.7.65/4.5.66
Class details: *Dp* 2,733 tons f.l. *Dm* 260 oa × 49 × $11\frac{1}{4}$ ft *My* 3 Paxman Ventura turbocharged diesels, 3,840bhp, 14 knots, 1 shaft *B/R* 450 tons/12,000 miles at 11 knots *Ct* 86. Can carry 1 Wasp helicopter

For reasons of space it is regretted that full details of **Royal Fleet Auxiliary** vessels cannot be included in this table; this is no reflection upon the vital part they played in the campaign. They are listed below:

Olmeda/A124, and **Olna/A123**, 22,300 dwt, 4 Sea King helicopters
Tidespring/A75, and **Tidepool/A76**, 17,400 dwt, 4 Sea King
Appleleaf/A79, **Bayleaf/A109** and **Brambleleaf/A81**, 33,000 dwt
Blue Rover/A270, 6,822 dwt, 1 Sea landing facilities
Pearleaf/A77, and **Plumleaf/A78**, 18,711 & 19,430 dwt respectively
Fort Austin/A386, and **Fort Grange/A385**, 8,160 dwt, 4 Sea King
Regent/A486, and **Resource/A480**, 18,029 grt, 4 Sea King
Stromness/A344, 7,782 dwt, 1 Sea King landing facilities
The Boom Defence Vessel **Goosander** and the tug **Typhoon** also took part in the campaign.

32 ASW torpedo tube; 1 or 2 Lynx helicopter *Ct* 223

Amazon Class:

Alacrity/F174 — *Bldr* Yarrow (SB) *LD/L/C* 5.3.73/18.9.74/2.7.77
Ambuscade/F172 — *Bldr* Yarrow (SB) *LD/L/C* 1.9.71/18.1.73/5.9.75
Antelope/F170 — *Bldr* Vosper Thorneycroft *LD/L/C* 23.3.71/16.3.72/19.7.75 **Sunk** 24.5.82

Ardent/F184 — *Bldr* Yarrow (SB) *LD/L/C* 26.2.74/9.5.75/13.10.77 **Sunk** 22.5.82
Arrow/F173 — *Bldr* Yarrow (SB) *LD/L/C* 28.9.72/5.2.74/29.7.76
Avenger/F185 — *Bldr* Yarrow (SB) *LD/L/C* 30.10.74/20.11.75/15.4.78

Class details: *Dp* 2,750 tons std. *Dm* 384 oa × $41\frac{3}{4}$ × $19\frac{1}{2}$ ft *My* 2 Rolls Royce Olympus TM3B gas turbines + 2 RR Tyne RM1A gas turbines, COGOG arrangement, 56,000bhp + 8,500bhp, 30 knots, 2 shafts *R* 4,000 miles at 17 knots *Arm* 4 × 1 Exocet SSM launcher; 1 × 4 Sea Cat SAM launcher; 1 × 1 4.5in. Mk 8 gun, 2 × 1 20mm Oerlikon; 2 × 3 ASW torpedo tube; 1 Lynx helicopter *Ct* 175

Leander Class:

Andromeda/F57 — *Bldr* Portsmouth DY *LD/L/C* 25.5.66/24.5.67/2.12.68 *Mod.* 12.80
Bacchante/F69 — *Bldr* Vickers-Armstrong *LD/L/C* 27.10.66/29.2.68/17.10.69

Class details: *Dp* 2,500 tons std., 2,962 f.l. *Dm* 372 oa × 43 × $14\frac{3}{4}$ ft *My* 2 double reduction geared steam turbines, 30,000shp, 28 knots, 2 shafts *B/R* 460 tons/4,000 miles at 15 knots *Arm: Andromeda*—4 × 1 Exocet SSM launcher; 1 × 6 Sea Wolf SAM launcher; 2 × 1 40mm gun; 2 × 3 Mk 32 ASW torpedo tube *Bacchante* 1 × 4 Sea Cat SAM launcher; 1 × 2 4.5in. Mk 6 gun, 2 × 1 20mm; 1 × 3 Limbo ASW mortar *Ct* 260

Leander Class, Batch II Modification:

Minerva/F45 — *Bldr* Vickers-Armstrong *LD/L/C* 25.7.63/19.12.64/14.5.66 *Mod.* 3.79
Penelope/F127 — *Bldr* Vickers-Armstrong *LD/L/C* 14.3.61/17.8.62/31.10.63 *Mod.* 3.81

Class details: *Dp* 2,450 tons std., 3,200 f.l. *Dm* 372 oa × 41 × $14\frac{3}{4}$ ft *My* 2 double reduction geared steam turbines, 30,000shp, 28 knots 2 shafts *B/R* 460 tons/4,000 miles at 15 knots *Arm* 4 × 1 Exocet SSM launcher; 3 × 4 Sea Cat SAM launcher; 2 × 1 40mm gun; 2 × 3 Mk 32 ASW torpedo tube; 1 Lynx helicopter *Ct* 223

Rothesay Class:

Plymouth/F126 — *Bldr* Devonport DY *LD/L/C* 1.7.58/20.7.59/11.5.61
Yarmouth/F101 — *Bldr* John Brown *LD/L/C* 29.11.57/23.3.59/26.3.60

Class details: *Dp* 2,380 tons std., 2,800 f.l. *Dm* 370 × 41 × $17\frac{1}{3}$ ft *My* 2 double reduction geared.steam turbines, 30,000shp, 30 knots, 2 shafts *B* 400 tons *Arm* 1 × 4 Sea Cat SAM launcher; 1 × 2 4.5in. Mk 6 gun; 1 × 3 Limbo ASW mortar; 1 Wasp helicopter *Ct* 235

SUBMARINES:

Churchill Class:

Conqueror/S48 — *Bldr* Cammell Laird *LD/L/C* 5.12.67/28.8.69/9.11.71 *Dp* 4,400 tons std., 4,900 submerged *Dm* 285 × $33\frac{1}{4}$ × 27 *My* 1 water-cooled nuclear reactor, 15,000shp, 28+ knots submerged, 1 shaft *Arm* 6 × 21in. torpedo tube, 32 torpedos *Ct* 103

Swiftsure Class:

Spartan/S105 — *Bldr* Vickers (SB) *LD/L/C* 26.4.76/7.4.78/22.9.79
Splendid/S106 — *Bldr* Vickers (SB) *LD/L/C* 23.11.77/5.10.79/21.3.81

Class details: *Dp* 4,200 tons std., 4,500 submerged *Dm* 272 × $32\frac{1}{3}$ × 27 ft *My* 1 water-cooled nuclear reactor, 15,000shp, 30+ knots submerged, 1 shaft *Arm* 5 × 21in. torpedo tube, 25 torpedos *Ct* 97

Oberon Class:

Onyx/S21 — *Bldr* Cammell Laird *LD/L/C* 16.11.64/18.8.66/20.11.67 *Dp* 1,610 tons syd., 2,410 submerged *Dm* $295\frac{1}{4}$ × $26\frac{1}{2}$ × 18 ft *My* 2 Admiralty diesels + 2 electric motors, 3,680bhp + 6,000shp, 12–17 knots, 2 shafts *Arm* 8 × 21in. torpedo tube, 24 torpedos *Ct* 69

AMPHIBIOUS WARFARE VESSELS:

Assault Ships:

Fearless/L10 — *Bldr* Harland & Wolff *LD/L/C* 25.7.62/19.12.63/25.11.65
Intrepid/L11 — *Bldr* John Brown *LD/L/C* 19.12.62/25.6.64/11.3.67

Class details: *Dp* 11,060 std., 12,120 f.l. *Dm* 520 oa × 80 × $20\frac{1}{2}$ ft *My* 2 English

ARGENTINE NAVY

AIRCRAFT CARRIER

Veinticinco de Mayo/V2 — *Bldr* Cammell Laird *LD/L/C* 3.12.42/30.12.43/17.1.45 *Dp* 15,892 tons std., 19,896 f.l. *Dm* $693\frac{1}{4}$ oa × 80 × 25 ft *My* 2 shaft geared Parsons steam turbines, 40,000shp, 24 knots, 4 3-drum boilers *B/R* 3,200 tons/12,000 miles at 14 knots *Arm* 9 × 1 40mm; a/c variable but normally 18 fixed-wing A-4Q, Tracker and/or Super-Etendard, 4 Alouette, Sea King helicopters *Ct* 1,000 + 500 air

CRUISER

General Belgrano/C4 (ex-Brooklyn Class) — *Bldr* New York SB *LD/L/C* 15.4.35/12.3.38/18.3.39 **Sunk** 2.5.82 *Dp* 10,800 tons std., 13,645 f.l. *Dm* $608\frac{1}{3}$ oa × 69 × 24 ft *My* Parsons geared turbines, 100,000shp, 32 knots, 4 shafts, 8 boilers *B/R* 2,200 tons/7,600 miles at 15 knots *P* Belt $1\frac{1}{2}$–4in., deck 3in., turrets 3–5in. *Arm* 5 × 3 15in., 4 × 2 5in., 2 × 2 40mm gun; 2 × 4 Sea Cat SAM launcher; 2 helicopters *Ct* 1,200

DESTROYERS:

ex-Allen M. Sumner Class:

Segui/D25 — *Bldr* Federal SB *LD/L/C* 17.1.44/21.5.44/28.8.44
Hipolito Bouchard/D26 — *Bldr* Federal SB *LD/L/C* 29.2.44/4.7.44/21.9.44
Piedra Buena/D29 — *Bldr* Bath Iron Wks *LD/L/C* 11.10.43/5.3.44/16.5.44

Class details: *Dp* 2,200 std., 3,320 f.l. *Dm* $376\frac{1}{2}$ × 41 × 19 ft *My* 2 geared steam turbines, 60,000shp, 34 knots, 2 shafts, 4 boilers *R* 4,600 miles at 15 knots *Arm* 4 × 1 Exocet SSM launcher; 3 × 2 5in. Mk 38 gun, 2 × 2 3in. Mk 33 gun (D25 only); 2 × 3 Ilas 3 ASW torpedo tube; 2 × Hedgehog ASW weapon; helicopter facilities (not D25) *Ct* 331 (D25), 291

ex-Gearing Class:

Comodoro Py/D27 — *Bldr* Con.Steel *LD/L/C* 7.12.44/3.45/5.4.45 *Dp* 2,425 tons std., 3,500 f.l. *Dm* $390\frac{1}{2}$ × $41\frac{1}{4}$ × 19 ft *My* 2 Westinghouse geared steam turbines, 60,000shp, $32\frac{1}{2}$ knots, 2 shafts *R* 5,800 miles at 15 knots *Arm* 4 × 1 Exocet SSM launcher; 3 × 2 5in. Mk 38 gun; 2 × 3 Ilas 3 ASW torpedo tube; 2 × Hedgehog ASW weapon; can land helicopter *Ct* 275

Type 42:

Hercules/D1
Santisima Trinidad — Details as British 'Sheffield' Class apart from addition of 4 × 1 Exocet SSM

FRIGATES:

Type A69:

Drummond/P1 — Completed 1978
Guerrico/P2 — Completed 1978
Granville/P3 — Completed 1981

Class details: *Dp* 950 tons std., 1,170 f.l. *Dm* $262\frac{1}{2}$ × $33\frac{3}{4}$ × $9\frac{3}{4}$ ft *My* 2 diesels, 11,000bhp, 24 knots, 2 shafts *R* 4,500 miles at 15 knots *Arm* 4 × 1 Exocet SSM launcher; 1 × 1 3.9in., 1 × 2 40mm, 2 × 1 20mm gun; 1 × 3 Mk 32 ASW torpedo tube *Ct* 93

SUBMARINES:

Guppy Class:

Santa Fe/S21 — *Bldr* Electric Boat *LD/L/C* ?/19.11.44/19.3.45 **CTL** 25.4.82
Santiago del Estero/S22? — Details unknown; both boats acquired 1971

Class details: *Dp* 1,870 tons std., 2,420 submerged *Dm* $307\frac{1}{2}$ × $27\frac{1}{4}$ × 18 ft *My* 2 diesels + 2 electric, 4,800 + 5,400shp, 18 knots surfaced, 15 knots submerged, 2 shafts *B/R* 300 tons/12,000 miles at 10 knots *Arm* 10 × 21in. torpedo tube *Ct* 82

Type 209:

Salta/S31 — *Bldr* Howaldtswerke *LD/L/C* 30.4.70/9.11.72/7.3.74
San Luis/S32 — *Bldr* Howaldtswerke *LD/L/C* 1.10.70/3.4.73/24.5.74

Class details: *Dp* 1,185 tons std., 1,285 submerged *Dm* $183\frac{1}{2}$ × $20\frac{1}{2}$ × 18 ft *My* MTU diesel + 4 electric gens. 5,000hp, 10 knots surfaced, 22 knots submerged, 1 shaft *Arm* 8 × 21in. torpedo tube, 14 torpedos *Ct* 32

In addition, we would list the briefest details of the Z-28 patrol craft (81 tons; 2 diesels, 22 knots, 1,200 miles; 2 × 1 20mm gun; 15 ct.) and the armed tugs (689 tons; diesel-electric, $12\frac{1}{2}$ knots, 16,500 miles; 1 × 1 40mm, 2 × 1 20mm gun; 49 ct.)

INDEX

(References to illustrations are shown in **bold**. Colour plates are prefixed 'pl.' with commentary locators in brackets, e.g. 'pl. **D** (24)'.)

COMPANION SERIES FROM OSPREY

ESSENTIAL HISTORIES
Concise studies of the motives, methods and repercussions of human conflict, spanning history from ancient times to the present day. Each volume studies one major war or arena of war, providing an indispensable guide to the fighting itself, the people involved, and its lasting impact on the world around it.

CAMPAIGN
Accounts of history's greatest conflicts, detailing the command strategies, tactics, movements and actions of the opposing forces throughout the crucial stages of each campaign. Full-colour battle scenes, 3-dimensional 'bird's-eye views', photographs and battle maps guide the reader through each engagement from its origins to its conclusion.

ORDER OF BATTLE
The greatest battles in history, featuring unit-by-unit examinations of the troops and their movements as well as analysis of the commanders' original objectives and actual achievements. Colour maps including a large fold-out base map, organisational diagrams and photographs help the reader to trace the course of the fighting in unprecedented detail.

ELITE
This series focuses on uniforms, equipment, insignia and unit histories in the same way as Men-at-Arms but in more extended treatments of larger subjects, also including personalities and techniques of warfare.

NEW VANGUARD
The design, development, operation and history of the machinery of warfare through the ages. Photographs, full-colour artwork and cutaway drawings support detailed examinations of the most significant mechanical innovations in the history of human conflict.

WARRIOR
Insights into the daily lives of history's fighting men and women, past and present, detailing their motivation, training, tactics, weaponry and experiences. Meticulously researched narrative and full-colour artwork, photographs, and scenes of battle and daily life provide detailed accounts of the experiences of combatants through the ages.

AIRCRAFT OF THE ACES
Portraits of the elite pilots of the 20th century's major air campaigns, including unique interviews with surviving aces. Unit listings, scale plans and full-colour artwork combine with the best archival photography available to provide a detailed insight into the experience of war in the air.

COMBAT AIRCRAFT
The world's greatest military aircraft and combat units and their crews, examined in detail. Each exploration of the leading technology, men and machines of aviation history is supported by unit listings and other data, artwork, scale plans, and archival photography.

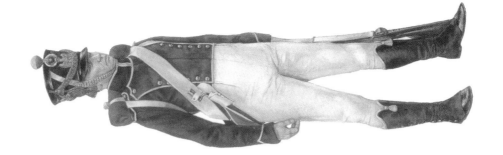

OSPREY PUBLISHING

FIND OUT MORE ABOUT OSPREY

❑ Please send me a FREE trial issue
  of Osprey Military Journal

❑ Please send me the latest listing of Osprey's publications

❑ I would like to subscribe to Osprey's e-mail newsletter

Title/rank

Name

Address

Postcode/zip   state/country

e-mail

Which book did this card come from?

❑ I am interested in military history

My preferred period of military history is _____

❑ I am interested in military aviation

My preferred period of military aviation is _____

I am interested in *(please tick all that apply)*

❑ general history ❑ militaria ❑ model making

❑ wargaming ❑ re-enactment

Please send to:

USA & Canada: Osprey Direct USA, c/o Motorbooks
International, P.O. Box 1, 729 Prospect Avenue, Osceola,
WI 54020

UK, Europe and rest of world:
Osprey Direct UK, P.O. Box 140, Wellingborough, Northants,
NN8 2FA, United Kingdom

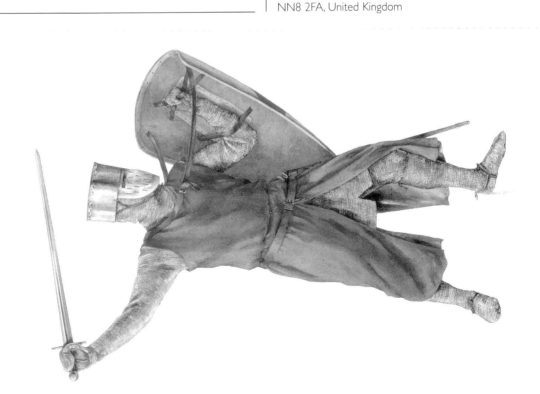

OSPREY
PUBLISHING

www.ospreypublishing.com

call our telephone hotline
for a free information pack

USA & Canada: 1-800-458-0454
UK, Europe and rest of world call:
+44 (0) 1933 443 863

Young Guardsman
Figure taken from *Warrior 22:
Imperial Guardsman 1799–1815*
Published by Osprey
Illustrated by Christa Hook

Knight, c.1190
Figure taken from *Warrior 1: Norman Knight 950 – 1204AD*
Published by Osprey
Illustrated by Christa Hook

POSTCARD